Southern Living

Walks, Walls & Patio Floors

The stone paving was carefully laid around a pattern for a love knot and a bow at each end. Dwarf mondo grass fills the meandering crevice with a ribbon of green.

Oxmoor House®

A darby helps you smooth wet concrete after it's poured and screeded. For details on laying a concrete slab, see pages 25–29.

Book Editor
Scott Atkinson

Coordinating Editor
Debby Thomas Kramer

Consulting Editor
Jane Horn

Editorial Coordinators
**Bradford Kachelhofer,
Vicki Weathers**

Design
Joe di Chiarro

Illustrations
Bill Oetinger

Photo Styling
JoAnn Masaoka Van Atta

Computer Production
Linda Bouchard

Photographers: Van Chaplin: 1, 24 top, 38 bottom left, 44, 45, 55 top, 58, back cover top right, back cover bottom right; **Peter Christiansen:** 42–43 bottom, 94; **Tina Cornett:** 21, back cover left; **Crandall & Crandall:** 23 top, 24 bottom, 69 bottom, 82, 86 left; **Claire Curran:** 38 bottom right; **Derek Fell:** 43 top, 79 bottom; **Philip Harvey:** 14 top right, 18, 23 bottom right, 37 bottom, 40, 48, 70, 74 bottom, 78, 79 top, 80 top, 83, 86 right, 89; **William Helsel:** 50 right; **Saxon Holt:** 55 bottom, 59 top, 74 top, 75 top, 84, 85 bottom; **Stephen Marley:** 68; **Sylvia Martin:** 11 top, 90, 95; **Jack Mc-Dowell:** 20, 50 center, 69 top, 80 bottom, 85 top; **Richard Nicol:** 13 bottom, 32 bottom, 37 top, 42 left, 49, 57, 59 bottom, 75 bottom, 91; **Don Normark:** 31 top, 38 top right; **Bill Ross:** 12 bottom, 22 right; **Michael Thompson:** 14 bottom; **Darrow M. Watt:** 10–11 bottom; **Peter O. Whiteley:** 22 left, 33, 50 left; **Russ Widstrand:** 13 top; **Cynthia Woodyard:** 14 top left, 23 bottom left; **Tom Wyatt:** 2, 4–5, 12 top, 26, 27, 30–31 bottom, 32 top, 36, 54 left, 62–63, 67.

The Basic Building Blocks

Walks, walls, and patios are the structural underpinnings of today's hardscapes. Besides stretching interior living space, a patio sets the stage for many outdoor activities. Walkways route traffic and double as borders, leading both eye and foot through the garden. Walls complete an outdoor room, carving out pockets of privacy and quiet.

Today's homeowner has more options than ever before. You'll see tinted concrete, earthy brick, jazzy interlocking pavers, and elegant flagstone tiles. What's best for your situation?

This book can answer such questions. It has two sections, one on patios and walks, another on walls. Both cover each popular building material, blending color photos with hands-on building instructions. Browse through the photo galleries and accompanying text for inspiration and shopping advice; then follow the step-by-step instructions on installation.

We're grateful to all the professionals and homeowners who shared their knowledge, enthusiasm, and garden designs with us. We'd particularly like to thank R. Scott Lankford, Lankford Associates of Seattle; Remick Associates; Peninsula Building Materials; and Bill McDougald of *Southern Living Magazine.*

Special thanks go to Marcia Morrill Williamson for carefully editing the manuscript and to Viki Marugg for her assistance in coloring the illustrations.

Southern Living® *Walks, Walls & Patio Floors* was adapted from a book by the same title published by Sunset Books.

Our appreciation to the staff of *Southern Living* magazine for their contributions to this book.

First printing January 2000
Copyright © 2000 by Oxmoor House, Inc.
Book Division of Southern Progress Corporation
P.O. Box 2463
Birmingham, Alabama 35201
All rights reserved, including the right of reproduction in whole or in part in any form.

Southern Living® is a federally registered trademark of Southern Living, Inc.

ISBN 0-376-09080-4
Library of Congress Catalog Card Number: 99-65020
Printed in the United States

Cover
Design: **James Boone, Vasken Guiragossian**

Photography: **Van Chaplin, Southern Progress Photo Collection.**

Landscape Architect: **Robert Chesnut**

CONTENTS

WALKS & PATIOS

Nothing brings indoor comfort outside like a new patio or walkway. And most paving skills are within the reach of a do-it-yourselfer. If you proceed carefully, the chief difference between you and the professional should be speed.

A first-rate job begins with careful site preparation. For grading and drainage pointers, see pages 6–7. Edgings, the borders that hold your paving in check, are discussed on pages 8–9.

You may find that a little local knowledge is a big help. Ask your building department or garden supplier about the best concrete mix, brick types, or base treatment for use with your climate and soil. Be sure to browse through local offerings before buying: new products appear constantly.

LAYING THE GROUNDWORK

No matter which paving you choose, you will probably have to prepare a foundation or subbase. The foundation will improve your patio's finished appearance and extend its life span. Since the paving material determines what kind of base you lay, this book's discussion of specific materials indicates the foundation requirements for each possibility.

In most situations, only minor leveling is necessary, though in some cases you may want to build a short retaining wall (see pages 90–93). However, the grading of certain sites — low-lying spots, steep slopes and hillsides, and areas with unstable soil, for example — can pose serious problems. In these cases, it's best to consult a landscape architect or landscape contractor.

Note: Be on the lookout for underground water, gas, or electrical lines running through your building site. These systems, plus lawn sprinklers or existing drains, may need rerouting before you can proceed.

Drainage

Whenever you pave an area, its drainage is affected, since water tends to run off even the most porous paving. Unless the site slopes naturally, it must be graded before paving so that runoff won't collect where it can cause problems — against a house foundation, for example. You should provide a pitch of at least 1 inch in 8 feet (or ⅛ inch per foot).

The bed you lay below the paving, whether sand or gravel, will often provide adequate drainage. But sometimes additional measures are necessary.

Perforated drainpipe. To draw off most of the water, you can place perforated plastic drainpipe in a narrow trench dug under the center or around the edge of the paved area. Dig the trench about 12 inches deep (deeper where the ground freezes) and lay the pipe, perforated side down, in the trench. Pack gravel around the pipe to

THREE DRAINAGE OPTIONS

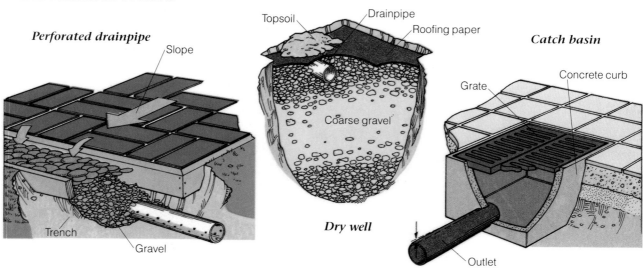

Perforated drainpipe — Slope, Trench, Gravel

Topsoil — Drainpipe — Roofing paper — Coarse gravel — *Dry well*

Catch basin — Concrete curb — Grate — Outlet

a depth of 6 inches and fill in above it. If the trench is under the patio site, keep the fill soaked for a few days to be sure it's properly packed.

Dry well. A dry well allows runoff water to soak into fast-draining soil. To build one, dig a 2- to 4-foot-wide hole at least 3 feet deep (keep the bottom above the water table). Next, dig trenches for drainpipes that will carry water into the dry well from other areas. Fill the hole with coarse gravel or small rocks and cover it with an impervious material, such as heavy roofing paper. Then conceal the well with topsoil.

Catch basin. To drain water from a low-lying area, use a catch basin, digging the hole for it at the lowest point. Set a precast concrete basin (available at building supply stores) into the hole, or form and pour the concrete base and sides yourself. Set a grate on top. Direct accumulated water toward a dry well, storm drain (if allowed), or gentle slope.

Final Grading

Once you've determined where to send the runoff, you're ready to start grading. Usually, this means digging out the area to be paved. Try to avoid filling and tamping; tamped earth is never as firm as undisturbed soil and will inevitably settle, taking your paving with it.

Drive stakes into the ground just beyond the patio corners, as shown above right. Next, mark the desired patio level on one stake for reference. Attach a length of twine to each stake, stretch it toward the adjacent stake, and level it with a line level (see page 18). Mark each stake where the twine crosses it.

To allow for the standard pitch (1 inch in 8 feet), figure your total drop and mark this on each corner stake below the level mark. Restring the perimeter lines at this level. To ensure a square layout, use the triangulation method shown, and measure diagonals.

To lay out an arc or circle, use a long board or straightedge. Stake or nail it to the ground at the center of the arc, measure off the radius, and pivot the board; mark the arc with builder's chalk or lime. Lay out free-form curves with a garden hose or rope, and check from all angles. Then mark the line and remove the hose.

Plan to leave a small gap where the paved surface meets a house or other structure. You'll want to install galvanized metal flashing to protect wood siding or floor framing from moisture damage.

Excavation. Working from the established perimeter, add more lines and stakes in 5-foot squares to use as reference points while digging.

LAYING OUT LINES

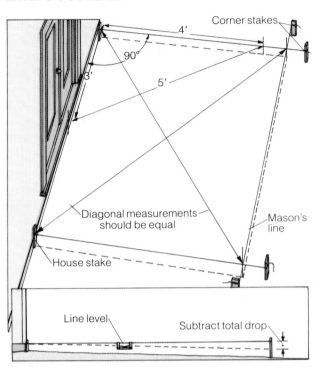

Corner stakes and mason's lines define patio perimeter; triangulation method and diagonal measurements help ensure it's square. Mark stakes for total drop (bottom inset), then restring perimeter.

Using a square-sided shovel and measuring down from the lines, excavate below them a distance equal to the paving thickness plus the thickness of the setting bed. Try to work parallel to the ground, removing the minimum amount of soil needed for the correct depth.

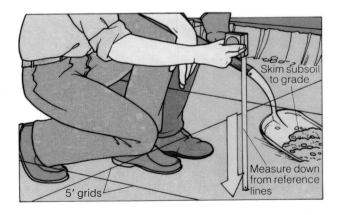

If you must even out a low spot, use decomposed granite, spreading it evenly with a rake; moisten it, then tamp it several times with a hand tamper or a rented power vibrator.

Edgings

Whether you lay it, hammer it, set it, or pour it in place, a patio or walkway almost always requires an edging. In addition to outlining the surface, the edging confines the pavement within the desired area — an important contribution when you're using loose materials, pouring concrete, or setting bricks in sand.

When used to curb paved areas, the edging is usually installed after the base has been prepared (see pages 6–7) and before the setting bed and paving are laid. Before you begin work, make sure you're familiar with the construction sequence for the specific paving material you're laying.

The mason's twine you strung around the perimeter of the area to be paved during grading marks the outside top border of the edging. To achieve the correct finished height, you'll probably have to dig narrow trenches under the lines.

Dimension-lumber edgings. The most popular edgings are made of 2 by 4 or 2 by 6 lumber; for special emphasis, you could use 4 by 4s or 6 by 6s. The installation sequence is shown above right. Choose pressure-treated lumber or the heartwood of cedar, redwood, or certain types of cypress.

Other wood edgings. Heavy timbers and railroad ties make strong, showy edgings and interior dividers, especially when drilled and threaded with steel pipe (see drawing below) or reinforcing rods.

In addition to rustic timbers, you can use wood posts or logs, in diameters ranging from 2 to 6 inches, to

INSTALLING WOOD EDGINGS

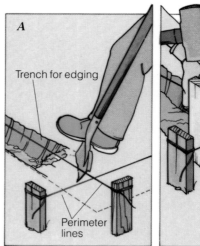

Standard wood edgings may require a narrow trench (A); dig below perimeter lines as shown. Then drive in 1 by 3 or 2 by 2 stakes flush with perimeter lines (B).

form a series of miniature pilings; set their bottoms in concrete, not in bare ground. For a more finished look, top off 4 by 4s with a horizontal 2 by 4 or 2 by 6 cap.

Curved wood edgings. For gentle curves, use flexible redwood benderboard. Soak it in water to make it more flexible. Then work it around guide stakes set on the inside edge of the curve, nailing or screwing the board to these stakes (see drawing below). For an outside curve, add stakes every 3 feet or so on the outside and fasten the benderboard to them; then pull up the inside stakes.

EIGHT MORE EDGINGS

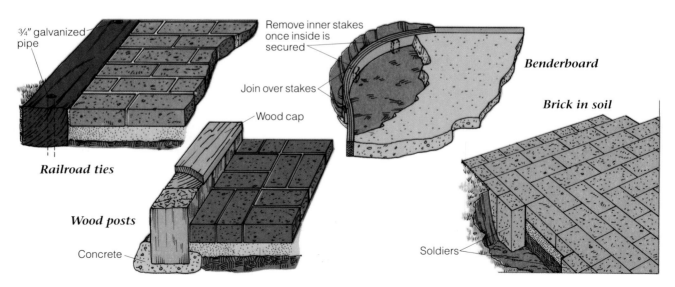

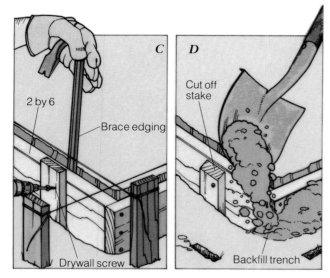

After fastening edging boards together, attach them to stakes as shown (C). Saw off exposed stakes at an angle; then pack excavated soil around the outside (D).

Bend additional boards around the first board, staggering any splices, until you've built up the curved edging to the same thickness as the straight sections. Nail all layers together between stakes with 2d (1-inch) nails.

Brick-in-soil edgings. You can set bricks vertically, horizontally, or, for a sawtooth effect, at a uniform angle. After grading the area to be paved, dig a narrow trench around the perimeter; make it deep enough so the tops of the bricks will be flush with the finished paving. Position the bricks, then pack soil around the outside.

Invisible edgings. An invisible edging secures paving units without any obvious support. Build temporary forms around the patio perimeter, as if for a concrete footing. Make the forms one brick-length wide in a trench deep enough to allow for a 4-inch concrete bed (deeper where the ground freezes).

Pour in concrete and, using a bladed screed, level it one brick thick below the top of the forms, as shown below. Place edging units in the wet concrete, butting their joints, and set them with a rubber mallet.

Flagstone. Before laying flagstones or other small stones, arrange them in a pleasing pattern, cutting them where necessary. Then lay the stones in 1-inch-thick mortar (see pages 46–47).

Uncut stone. Larger rocks and boulders usually look best if they're partially buried; otherwise, prop them up with smaller rocks, then pack the area with soil and plantings. Cut formal paving units or wood decking to fit around boulders.

Preformed edgings. Manufactured plastic or aluminum edgings are easy to install. The strips secure bricks or concrete pavers below finished paving height; you then conceal them with soil or sod. Flexible sections can negotiate tight curves.

Concrete edgings. Concrete can work like an invisible edging. Construct forms, pour the concrete, then screed it flush with the top of the forms so the edging will be even with the paved surface. Finish the concrete as desired (for ideas, see pages 26–27) and let it cure.

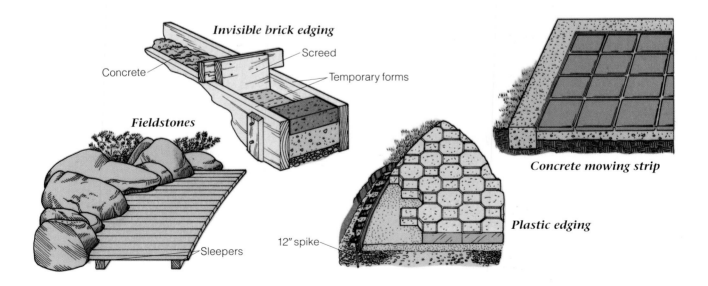

BRICK PAVING

Brick is the most frequently chosen patio surfacing material available, and probably the most adaptable. Set on sand or in mortar, it provides a handsome, nonglare surface that blends with nearly any architectural style and looks at ease in almost any setting. Today, brick is available in an almost unlimited range of colors, sizes, and finishes.

Brick does have disadvantages. Cost per square foot runs higher than that of many alternative materials. If bricks are carelessly installed, the resultant pavement can be jarringly uneven. Also, when set in a moist, heavily shaded area, bricks can develop an algaelike surface growth that makes them dangerously slick.

Brick Types

Of the bewildering variety turned out by brickyards, two basic kinds are used for garden paving: rough-textured common brick and slick-surfaced face brick.

Most garden paving is done with common brick. People like its familiar color and texture, and it has the undoubted advantage of being less expensive than face brick. Common bricks are more porous than face bricks and less uniform in size and color (they may vary as much as ¼ inch in length).

Face brick is not as widely available as common brick; you'll notice it is used more often for facing walls and buildings than for residential paving. It can, however, make attractive accents, edgings, header courses, stair nosings, and raised beds. Use it where its smoothness won't present a safety hazard.

Used brick has uneven surfaces and streaks of old mortar that can look very attractive in an informal

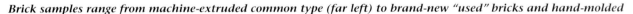

Brick samples range from machine-extruded common type (far left) to brand-new "used" bricks and hand-molded

For privacy from the street and neighbors, a 6-foot-high brick wall encloses a matching brick terrace. Landscape architect: Brian Zimmerman.

ones (far right). Color comes from chemical composition of clay and firing method and temperature.

pavement. Manufactured used or "rustic" bricks cost about the same as the genuine article and are easier to find; they're also more consistent in quality than most older bricks.

Low-density firebricks, blond-colored and porous, provide interesting accents but don't wear well as general paving.

Precut brick, another option, is a boon for the do-it-yourselfer venturing out into more complicated brick-laying patterns. Expect to pay about the same per unit as for a full-size brick.

The standard modular brick is about 8 inches long by 4 inches wide by 2⅜ inches thick. Other modular units may be available at larger brick-yards, in sizes ranging from 12 by 4 by 2 inches to 12 by 8 by 4 inches.

"Paver" bricks are roughly half the thickness of standard bricks. "True" or "mortarless" pavers are a standard 4 by 8 inches (plus or minus ⅛ inch) and can be a big help when you're laying a complex pattern with closed (tightly butted) joints.

All outdoor bricks are graded by their ability to withstand weathering; if you live where it freezes and thaws, buy only those graded SW (severe weathering).

Shopping for Brick

You can find many brick types at masonry suppliers or building and landscape supply yards; look in the yellow pages of your telephone directory under "Brick" or "Building Materials." When you order, ask about delivery charges; though usually low, they're often not included in the quoted price. Paying a little more to have the bricks delivered on a pallet prevents the considerable breakage that can result when the bricks are merely dumped off a truck.

To calculate the quantities of brick you'll need for your project, visit your building supplier first, measuring tape in hand.

Colorful peacock pattern lends visual punch to a small backyard. Such "renaissance" patterns require skilled cutting, unless you can find an outlet for precut bricks. Landscape contractor: Richard Casavecchia/Architectural Garden Specialties.

Only partially grouted, basket-weave pattern (below) allows growing space for purple alyssum and other small plants.

Blue-gray entry walk, mortared in 45° herringbone pattern, is set off by beige concrete dividers. Landscape architect: Mark Scott Associates.

Mortared bricks, laid in running bond, lead toward wider patio with flagstone inserts. Field bricks were trimmed to short length; contrasting border units are placed on edge. Landscape architect: The Berger Partnership, P.S.

Ungrouted gaps in brick pool surround allow runoff water to reach drainage channel below. Landscape architect: Royston, Hanamoto, Alley & Abey.

Fish accent swims in a whorled frame at the center of mortared brick patio. All pieces are standard brick cut in custom shapes and sizes; varying grout spaces accommodate curves. Design: Cynthia Woodyard.

Walkway of salvaged brick is a refreshing alternative to typically linear walks. Because these units are mortared, irregular edgings can run "wild" into surrounding garden.

HOW TO LAY BRICK

Building with brick is pleasant work. The units are sized for easy one-hand lifting, and bricklaying takes on a certain rhythm once you get the hang of it. Even the tools and techniques are basic and non-threatening.

Paving methods include brick in sand, dry mortar, and wet mortar. The first is the easiest technique for beginners; dry mortar is a variation on the brick-in-sand method. The wet mortar method, which produces the most formal-looking results, is best left to experienced do-it-yourselfers.

Patio Patterns

When choosing a brick pattern (also known as a bond), consider the degree of difficulty involved. Some bonds require not only accuracy but also a lot of cutting of bricks. The patterns shown are some of the most popular; the jack-on-jack and running bonds are simplest to lay.

Your choice of bond will also be affected by whether you plan to lay the bricks with closed joints (butted together) or open joints (spaced).

Variations in the sizes of common clay bricks can make some patterns difficult to complete if the bricks are to be tightly butted; a jack-on-jack pattern, for example, would be hard to maintain over a large area. And when laid solid, a basket-weave pattern produces a curious effect: a

BASIC BRICK PATTERNS

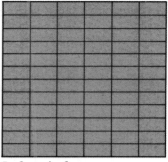
Jack on jack

Running bond

Basket weave

Half basket weave

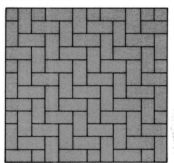
Herringbone

Pinwheel

½-inch hole appears at the center of each block of eight bricks. Where closed joints are required, consider more uniform paver bricks (choose "true" or "mortarless" pavers).

Before you build, lay out your design on graph paper, making allowances for joints as desired. You might buy a few sample bricks to try out at home. Or cut out cardboard shapes and arrange them on the ground. Don't be afraid to use your imagination—but take care not to make the pattern too busy, especially if you're paving a small area.

When you pave a large area in a single bond, the look can become monotonous. To avoid this problem, try changing the direction of the bond to vary it, or combine two patterns. Mixing brick colors—alternating light and dark within simple patterns, mixing colors and patterns, or creating a special border treatment—also adds design interest.

Another effective touch is to work with a grid system of redwood, concrete, or railroad ties. The building technique is the same as with edgings; see pages 8–9.

HOW TO CUT A BRICK

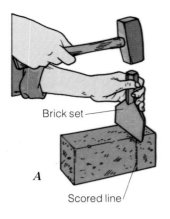

A — Brick set — Scored line

B — Bevel toward waste

To trim a brick, use a brick set to score a line on all four sides (A); make the cut with one sharp blow (B).

Cutting Bricks

No matter how carefully you plan, some cutting is almost inevitable. Plan to do this work all at once, after you're certain of exact sizes.

If you have just a few cuts to make, the best tool is a chisel-like implement called a brick set. Lay the brick to be cut on flat sand and place the chisel (with its bevel facing away from the piece to be used) along the cut line (see drawing above left). Tap the chisel sharply with a hand sledge or soft-headed hammer (wear safety glasses). For cleaner results, tap the brick lightly to score a groove across all four sides before administering the final blow. If necessary, chip away the

rough edges with the brick set or a mason's hammer.

If you have a lot of cutting to do, a diamond-bladed tub saw (see page 34) is your best bet. Rent one for the day from a masonry supplier or tool rental outlet.

Site Preparation

Successful bricklaying depends on proper preparation of the base. The ground should be solid. If you have to lay bricks on fill, be sure it has settled for some time, preferably a year. The fill must be wetted and tamped or rolled before you lay the bricks. A bit of dry cement will help hold fill in place.

You can also lay brick on an existing concrete slab that's clean and in good condition.

Carefully study the root systems of any aggressively growing plants, especially if you're planning to lay bricks in mortar or if you're using a grid system. Exceptionally vigorous roots can disturb the best-laid walk or patio. You may want to remove invasive plants, or design around them.

Then lay out the base grade (see page 7), taking into account the base required for the bricklaying technique you've chosen (see below). If drainage is poor, you may also need to add a 4-inch gravel base (where the ground freezes, 6 to 8 inches is advisable). Placing a layer of filter fabric over the gravel is optional; the fine mesh prevents the growth of weeds.

It's best to give a firm edge to this kind of paving, both for appearance and for permanent stability. Dimension lumber, railroad ties, invisible edgings, and poured-concrete edgings (see pages 8–9) all work well for brick patios. If you're installing a curved brick edging, adjust joint spaces as required to take the bends.

Laying Bricks in Sand

A brick-in-sand patio is one of the easiest paving projects for a beginner. With careful preparation and installation, this surface is as durable as bricks set in mortar and as permanent as you want it to be. An added advantage: if you decide to change the patio later, you need destroy only one brick to get the rest out in perfect condition.

Typically, a bed of 1½- to 2-inch-thick sand or rock fines (a mix of grain sizes) is prepared and the bricks are laid with closed joints. You can set them with open joints, but the surface will be less stable. The bricks can work loose as the sand settles, requiring that joints be refilled from time to time. (But if you're using bricks which vary considerably in

A SOLID BASE FOR BRICKS

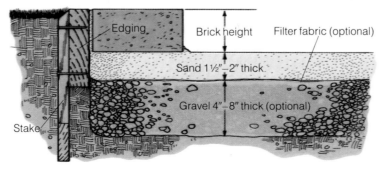

Edging · Brick height · Filter fabric (optional)

Sand 1½"–2" thick

Gravel 4"–8" thick (optional)

Stake

Typical brick-in-sand patio includes gravel bed, filter fabric, packed sand, and wood edging.

size, open joints may be the only answer.)

Grading the base. Lay out the base grade as discussed on page 7. You don't need absolute perfection—the sand will take care of slight irregularities in the leveling process. Dump the gravel (if you're using it), rake it out evenly, and then tamp it down.

Edging. Build permanent wood or masonry edgings around the perimeter to hold both bricks and sand firmly in place. Or use temporary wood forms to hold a poured-concrete edging until it hardens. For edge-building details, see pages 8–9.

If your design calls for one, add a permanent grid system. Plan to lay a sample section before installing the permanent grid so you can check fit and minimize brick-cutting.

Screeding. A key operation is leveling the sand to create a uniform surface on which the bricks will rest. To accomplish this, a "screed" is pulled along edgings or temporary guides, leveling the sand as it goes.

Make the screed from a 2 by 4; then nail on a plywood extension that's 3 inches or so shorter on both ends than the 2 by 4 and, for most edgings, slightly less than one brick's thickness wider. For a wide patio where the screed won't reach between edgings, use a temporary guide (a board or pipe) on which to rest one end of the screed.

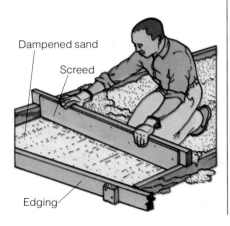

Dampened sand

Screed

Edging

Spread dampened sand in the first section and screed it smooth and level, using a sawing motion as you go. For a good, firm base, tamp the sand after screeding; add more sand, if needed, and screed again. An optional pass with a steel trowel can create an extra-smooth surface. Don't walk on the base after the final screeding or troweling.

Setting bricks. Stretch a mason's line between edgings to aid in alignment, and use a level often as you lay the bricks. Working from one corner and following the pattern you've chosen, gently set the bricks into position, making sure they fit as planned. (Don't slide them—you'll displace sand from the bed and trap it between bricks.)

Mason's line

Lightly tap each brick into place with a mallet or hammer handle. If a brick is twisted, realign it with a trowel blade. If it's too low, pry it out and add more sand.

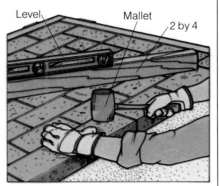

Level   Mallet

2 by 4

Adding sand. When all the bricks are placed to your satisfaction, you're ready to fill in the joints. Throw fine sand out over the surface and let it dry for a few hours; then sweep it into the cracks.

Fine sand

Wet the area with a light spray so the sand in the joints settles completely. If necessary, repeat the process.

Laying Bricks with Dry Mortar

If you like the idea of open joints in brickwork but would prefer not having to rework the patio from time to time, consider the dry mortar method. The bricks are set the same way as bricks in sand with open joints, but you add portland cement to the sand that is swept into the joints and then gently wet down the surface.

Although dry mortar isn't difficult to work with, some will usually stick to the bricks when you sweep, leaving a stain. This may not be a disadvantage if you like a rustic look.

Placing bricks and mortar. Following the directions for bricks in sand, lay and screed the sand bed; then set the bricks, leaving ½-inch joints (use ½-inch plywood and a mason's line for alignment). Check frequently with a level.

Prepare a dry mortar mix of 1 part cement and 4 parts sand. Kneel-

Tools of the Trade

To join the home mason's ranks, you need a few tools. A quick search of your workshop or garage may turn up a good number of them: a hammer, a saw, a 2-foot carpenter's level, a carpenter's square, a steel measuring tape, and a rubber mallet.

Some additional tools (shown below) will make the job go more smoothly. Mason's twine is useful for laying out perimeter lines or guides for straight courses; corner blocks help hold the lines in place. A small line level and a mason's level are helpful for checking over a large area.

A brick set or a broad-bladed cold chisel can be used for cutting and dressing bricks. Drive it with a hand sledge or a soft-headed hammer. For most jobs involving mortar, you'll need a pointed trowel with a 10-inch blade.

For concrete surfacing, you will need a bull float or darby to float the concrete, a wooden float and/or rectangular steel trowel to finish the concrete surface, an edger to form smooth edges, and a jointer to cut control joints.

You may also want to invest in some optional masonry paraphernalia: a couple of jointers to shape mortar joints; a mason's hammer to chip rough edges away from a cut brick, block, or stone; and a pair of brick tongs to help lug heavy masonry units.

You may be able to rent these tools locally. Also, rent any needed heavy equipment, such as a concrete mixer, drum roller, plate vibrator, or tub saw. You can even rent concrete forms or stamping tools in some areas.

Masonry tools are few and straightforward. For brick and other units, you'll need a pointed trowel (1), plus a brick set (2), mason's hammer (3), and hand sledge (4) for making cuts. Jointers (5) smooth grout joints. Corner block (6) and mason's twine (7) help keep you on course; so do line level (8), plumb bob (9), and 4-foot mason's level (10). Ready for concrete work? You'll want a darby (11) or bull float, wooden float (12) and/or steel trowel (13), edger (14), and jointer (15). Brick tongs (16) make it easier to lug units from place to place.

ing on a piece of plywood (to avoid disturbing the bricks), spread the mixture over the surface, brushing it into the joints.

Tamp the mortar firmly with a piece of ½-inch plywood to improve the bond, adding more mix if needed. Carefully sweep and dust the bricks before continuing. Any mix that remains may leave stains.

Dry mortar mix
½" plywood

Wetting the surface. Using an extremely fine spray, wet the paving. Don't allow pools to form, and don't splash the mortar out of the joints. During the next several hours, wet the paving periodically to keep it damp.

When the mortar begins to harden, you can smooth, or rake, the joints with a concave jointer or another rounded object to give the job a professional look. For information on removing excess mortar from the bricks, see "Grouting the joints," at right.

Laying Bricks in Wet Mortar

Setting brick paving in mortar is a trickier job. The method used by professionals—buttering each brick before putting it in place—requires much practice. But there's another procedure, by which even the relative beginner can achieve handsome results. For general guidelines on mixing and working with mortar, see page 67.

Preparing the bed. You can either start with an existing concrete slab (it must be clean and in good condition) or pour a new foundation (for help, turn to pages 25–29). Ask your brick supplier if you need to prepare the concrete before adding the bricks.

Preparing a mortar bed. Add edgings, as described on pages 8–9; they should extend one brick's thickness plus ½ inch (the thickness of the mortar bed) above the slab.

Wet the bricks several hours before you plan to use them (to prevent them from sucking the water out of the mortar mixture). To make the mortar, mix 1 part portland cement and 3 parts sand, plus an optional ½ part hydrated lime to improve workability. Gradually add enough water so the mortar spreads easily but doesn't run. Mix only as much mortar as you can use in an hour.

Then lay and screed a ½-inch-thick mortar bed between the edgings (add temporary guides where necessary). The screed should ride on the edgings and extend one brick's thickness below them, as shown below. Screed only about 10 square feet at a time.

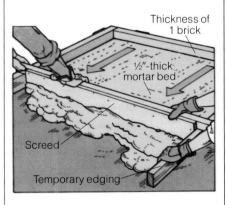

Thickness of 1 brick
½"-thick mortar bed
Screed
Temporary edging

Setting the bricks. Place the bricks in your chosen pattern, leaving ½-inch joints between them (use a piece of ½-inch plywood for a spacer and a mason's line for alignment). Gently tap each brick with a rubber mallet or hammer handle and check frequent-

ly with a level. Wait 24 hours before finishing the joints.

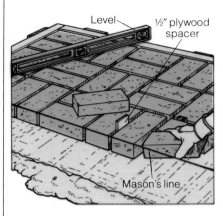

Level
½" plywood spacer
Mason's line

Grouting the joints. Use a pointed trowel to pack mortar (the same mix as for the bed) into the joints, working carefully to keep mortar off the bricks. When the mortar begins to harden (about 30 minutes), you can smooth the joints with a concave jointer or another rounded object.

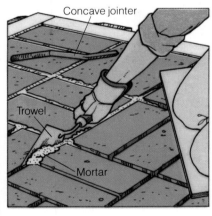

Concave jointer
Trowel
Mortar

Let the mortar set for about 2 hours; then scrub each brick with a wet burlap sack. Should further cleaning be necessary, wash the bricks with a solution of ½ cup each trisodium phosphate and laundry detergent in a gallon of water. Rinse well with clean water.

Keep the mortar damp for about 24 hours by covering the bricks with a plastic sheet. Stay off the paving for 3 days.

CONCRETE PAVING

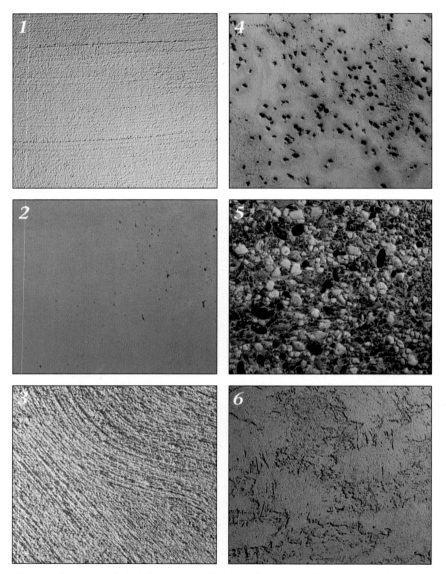

Shown above are six basic concrete finishes. Semismooth texture (1) is achieved with a wooden float; slick troweled surface (2) is suitable for covered patios; broomed surface (3) is best where maximum traction is needed. Rock salt (4), exposed aggregate (5), and travertine (6) are three popular decorative finishes.

Though sometimes disparaged as cold and forbidding, poured concrete is even more variable in appearance than brick. Used with the proper forms, it can conform to almost any shape. It can be lightly smoothed or heavily brushed; surfaced with handsome pebbles; swirled or scored; tinted or painted; patterned; or molded to resemble another material. And if you get tired of the concrete surface later on, you can use it as a foundation for a new pavement of brick, stone, or tile set in mortar.

Concrete does have disadvantages. In some situations it can seem harsh, hot, glaring, or simply boring. If smoothly troweled, concrete can become slick when wet. And once its dry ingredients are combined with water, you have to work fast; a mistake could require an extensive and perhaps costly redo.

Shopping for Materials

Concrete is a mixture of portland cement, sand, aggregate, and water. Cement is the "glue" that binds everything together and gives the finished product its hardness. The sand and aggregate (usually gravel) act as fillers and control shrinkage.

Depending on how much time and money you're willing to invest, you can make up your own concrete mix from scratch, buy dry or wet ready-mix, or order transit-mix from a concrete company. If your project is fairly large, ordering materials in bulk

and mixing them yourself is the economical way to go. Buying bagged, dry ready-mix concrete is expensive, but it's also convenient, especially for small jobs. On a grander scale, some dealers supply trailers, containing 1 cubic yard of wet ready-mix concrete (about enough for an 8- by 10-foot patio), that you can haul with your car. For a larger patio, a commercial transit-mix truck can deliver enough concrete to allow you to finish your project in a single pour.

To locate concrete plants, look in the yellow pages under "Concrete—Ready-Mixed."

Surface Treatments

Concrete pavings are typically given some type of surface treatment, both for appearance's sake and to provide traction.

You can wash or sandblast a concrete paving to uncover the aggregate, or embed colorful pebbles and stones in it (this finish, generally known as exposed aggregate, is probably the most popular contemporary paving surface).

Other ways to modify the standard steel-troweled concrete surface include color-dusting, staining, masking, sandblasting, acid-washing, and salt-finishing. You or a professional can also stamp and tint concrete to resemble stone, tile, or brick. The patterns simulate either butted joints or open ones, which can then be grouted to look like unit masonry.

Combining concrete and brick is popular; and tile and flagstone are other materials that complement concrete. Wood, steel, or copper dividers can be used to act as control joints to help prevent cracking. These materials also allow you to divide the job into smaller, more manageable pours.

Freeform shapes resembling giant stepping-stones were dug into the soil and then filled with concrete. Plantings between pads soften the overall look. Landscape architect: Katzmaier Newell Kehr.

Scored and tinted concrete, river gravel, and colorful dwarf plantings replace former lawn. Landscape architect: Josephine Zeitlin.

Creating a Softer Look

Special techniques can allow concrete to be used pleasingly in a more casual environment. For a natural look, leave planting pockets in a freshly poured slab, filling them with soil and plants. Drip tubing can be routed to these pockets to water planted areas regularly without soaking the surrounding paving.

Or dig holes or shape curved forms and fill them with concrete. The resulting pads — with planting spaces in between — can be textured, smoothed, or seeded with aggregate.

Exposed aggregate, though justly popular, can look forbidding in large doses. Design at top creates interest by alternating patches of light/dark and small/large pebbles. Edging boulders (below right) also help soften large expanse and blend concrete with its surroundings. Landscape contractor (boulders): Grimes Natural Landscape, Inc.

These aggregate pads were cast individually, then set into packed bed. Pathway doubles as edging, dividing lawn from planting beds. Design: Susan Ryley.

Now a colorful courtyard, this enclosed condo patio was originally stark, white, and uninviting concrete. The material hasn't changed, but it's been stained a muted, sandy color for more interest. Landscape architect: Terry Lewis.

Fish-scale pattern is one of many concrete stamping possibilities. Spaces between scales may be left open or grouted to simulate tile, brick, or other masonry units.

HOW TO POUR CONCRETE

The trick with concrete is to start small. Getting ready for the pour will probably take more time than actually pouring and finishing the concrete.

Plan to divide your work into stages that you and one or two other people can handle effectively—you won't have a contractor's specialized equipment and large crew. Pour large areas in sections or cast only a few paving pads at a time. If you're not sure you want to tackle the pour, you may be able to do site preparation yourself, then ask professionals to take over.

Choosing a Formula

Use this formula for regular concrete (the proportions are by volume):

> 1 part cement
> 2½ parts sand
> 2½ parts aggregate
> ½ part water

The sand should be clean construction sand (not beach sand). The aggregate should range from quite small to about ¾ inch in size. The water should be drinkable — neither excessively alkaline nor acidic, and containing no organic matter.

In areas with severe freeze-thaw cycles, you'll need to add an air-entraining agent to the basic formula.

This creates billions of tiny air bubbles in the finished concrete, which help it to expand and contract without cracking. The agent also makes concrete more workable; and, because you add less water, the finished paving is often stronger. Ask your supplier how much agent to add to your concrete formula.

For every 10 cubic feet of finished concrete, you'll need the following amounts of dry ingredients: 2½ sacks of cement, 5 cubic feet of sand, and 7 cubic feet of gravel. If you're using ready-mix, buy ⅓ cubic yard for every 10 cubic feet.

Preparing for the Pour

Like any paving, concrete requires a stable, well-drained base. And because the finished slab is monolithic, it's especially important to ensure that the ground beneath it won't shift and cause the concrete to crack.

Lay out and grade the site (for help, see pages 6–7). If the exposed soil is soft, wet it and then tamp it firmly. The standard slab for pathways and patios is 4 inches thick. In addition, plan on at least a 2-inch gravel base in areas where frost and drainage are not problems, and a 4- to 8-inch base where they are.

Building & Placing Forms

Forms are built the same way as wood edgings (see pages 8–9). Wet concrete exerts a lot of pressure, so forms should be strong and securely anchored to the ground. For standard paving, use 2 by 4s on edge for forms and 12-inch 1 by 3s or 2 by 2s for stakes. Screw or nail the forms to the stakes at least every 4 feet. Driving the stakes slightly below the surface of the forms will make placing and finishing the concrete easier.

If you plan to leave the form lumber in place as permanent edgings and dividers, use rot-resistant redwood, cedar, or cypress, or pressure-treated lumber. Drive 16d galvanized nails partway into the form about every 18 inches (see drawing below); this will lock the boards to the slab.

For curved forms, use tempered hardboard or plywood; you may

CONCRETE SLAB OVERVIEW

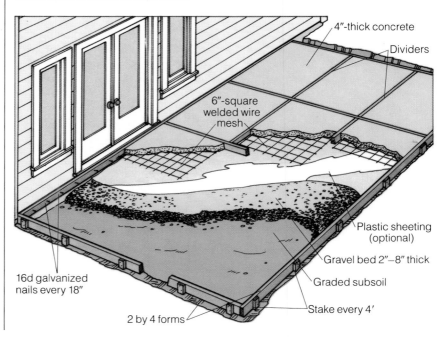

- 4"-thick concrete
- Dividers
- 6"-square welded wire mesh
- Plastic sheeting (optional)
- Gravel bed 2"–8" thick
- Graded subsoil
- Stake every 4'
- 16d galvanized nails every 18"
- 2 by 4 forms

Jazzing Up Concrete

As demonstrated on pages 20–24, the appearance of a concrete surface can be altered to suit a variety of tastes. You have two basic options (they can also be combined): texturing and coloring. Here are some of the most widely used techniques.

Sprinkle pebbles over freshly poured slab; press into place with a wooden float. Later, brush away excess concrete while wetting with a fine spray.

Exposed-aggregate finish

This attractive finish is a favorite for residential concrete work. To achieve it, pour the slab in the usual manner, but level it about ½ inch lower than the form boards. Then add the variegated smooth pebbles that make this finish so popular, distributing them evenly in a single layer over the slab. Using a block of wood, a float, or a darby, press the pebbles down until they lie just below the surface of the concrete. Refloat the concrete.

When the slab begins to harden, gently brush or broom the surface while wetting it down with a fine spray. Stop when the tops of the stones show. Any cement left on the stones can be removed later with a 10 percent muriatic acid solution.

Salt finish

To produce a distinctive pocked surface, scatter coarse chunks of rock salt over the concrete after it has been floated; then press the salt in with a float or trowel and wait for the water

sheen to disappear. Depending on the smoothness you desire, finish the surface by troweling or wood floating. After curing the slab, simply wash out the salt with a strong spray of water. (This finish is not recommended for areas with severe winters. Water trapped in the pockets will expand upon freezing and may crack or chip the surface.)

Travertine finish

For a marbled effect, try a travertine finish — but not if you live where the ground freezes.

After striking and floating the concrete, roughen the surface slightly with a broom — or just leave it very roughly floated. Then, using a large brush, dash a 1:2 cement-sand mix unevenly over the surface. Color the mixture to contrast with the concrete for a heightened effect.

When the slab can support you on knee boards, float or trowel the surface, knocking down the high spots. The result is a texture smooth in the high spots and rougher in the low spots.

CURVED FORMS

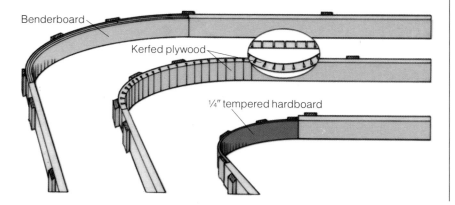

Benderboard

Kerfed plywood

¼" tempered hardboard

need extra stakes to ensure adequate support. For very tight curves, cut sheet metal, plastic, or another flexible material to size and fasten it to the stakes. If the curved form is to remain in place, layer redwood benderboard around the stakes until the thickness is equal to your other form boards.

Temporary forms should be oiled to aid in stripping; use motor oil or a commercial release agent. Cover tops of permanent forms with waterproof masking tape to prevent them from getting stained by the concrete.

Stamping or tooling

Stamping can make a concrete slab resemble brick, adobe, or stone. The technique is simple, at least for a contractor. First, a regular concrete slab is poured and floated smooth.

After floating, a special grid of patterned stamps is pressed into the slab; workers stand on the grids to force them into the concrete. A final going-over with a trowel fixes any blemishes. The stamped "joints" can be left as is or mortared to resemble regular mortar joints.

Coloring concrete

To add color to paving, you can mix color pigments into wet concrete before it's poured, dust color pigment on the surface during the finishing process, or apply stain or paint to the paving after it's completely cured.

Mix-in color. Mix the pigment with the cement and aggregate in a dry state first. Using white portland cement will produce brighter coloration; reserve standard cement for black and dark tones.

With this method, you can either pour an entire slab of colored concrete mixture or pour a conventional slab first, leaving the surface rough, and then cover it with a 1-inch slab of the colored mix.

Dust-on color. To apply color this way, first prepare the concrete surface through the wood-floating process; then spread two-thirds of the amount of color specified by the manufacturer and float the surface. Apply the remaining mixture, float again, and finish with a light troweling.

Brush-on color. Use this method to apply color to a concrete surface after it has cured at least six weeks. Scrub the surface with a solution of trisodium phosphate and warm water (be sure to wear gloves). Then flush with clear water.

Chemical stains (water-based solutions of metallic salts) create mottled colors that have a rich, translucent patina. Semitransparent wood stains also work well on concrete. Apply stain with a roller or brush; add a second coat to deepen the color.

Add powdered pigment to dry concrete ingredients before mixing. This 1-inch color layer is being screeded atop a standard slab; you could also tint the entire pour.

Though less durable than stains, paints provide the widest choice in colors. Choose from deck paint, tennis-court paint, or other exterior formulations. After cleaning the surface, you may want to etch it with a 10 percent muriatic acid solution. Roll or brush on two or three coats of paint.

Reinforcement

Reinforcing a concrete area more than 8 feet square with steel mesh can help prevent cracking and hold the pieces together if cracking does occur; 6-inch-square welded mesh is most commonly used.

Install the mesh after the forms are ready. Cut it to size with bolt cutters or heavy pliers, keeping it several inches away from the sides of the forms. If necessary, wire pieces together with a 6-inch overlap. Support

the mesh on small stones, bits of brick, or broken concrete so that it will be held midway in the slab.

Instead of steel reinforcement, you might install expansion strips (available at building supply centers) every 10 feet or less. Or you can pour the paving in modules formed by a grid of 2 by 4 dividers to allow for settling and expansion.

If you're not sure whether or not you need reinforcement, consult your building department or a landscape professional.

WIRE MESH DETAIL

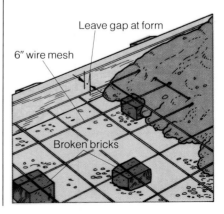

Leave gap at form

6" wire mesh

Broken bricks

Mixing Concrete

If you're mixing your own concrete, you can do it either by hand or with a power mixer. For small projects, hand-mixing is undoubtedly the simplest method. But large forms that must be filled in a single pour may warrant the use of a power mixer. If you're using air-entrained concrete, you must have a power mixer: hand-mixing is simply not sufficiently vigorous to create enough air bubbles.

Hand-mixing. A high-sided wheelbarrow is adequate for mixing 3 cubic feet at a time. For larger batches, use a simple wooden platform or a mortar box (one measuring 53 by 25 by 11 inches will handle up to 6 cubic feet of concrete).

Ingredients for small quantities of concrete are usually measured with a shovel—an accurate enough method if your scoopfuls are consistent. Or empty a sack of cement into a bucket, level it, and then mark the bucket; this equals 1 cubic foot. If you also mark the bucket for ½ cubic foot, you'll find it easier to fill.

Mark a bucket off in quarts and gallons to keep track of the water. Set up so you can bail water from a metal or plastic drum or garbage can; it's more convenient than turning a hose on and off.

Measure the sand, spread it evenly, and spread the cement on top. Turn and mix the dry ingredients until no streaks of color appear. Add gravel or rock and mix until evenly distributed. Then make a depression in the mixture and slowly add water, turning the ingredients until they're thoroughly combined. Use a rolling motion with a shovel or hoe.

Work your test batch with a trowel. The concrete should slide—not run—freely off the trowel, and you should be able to smooth the surface fairly easily, submerging the larger aggregates.

If your mix is stiff and crumbly, add a little water. If it's wet and soupy,

add a mixture of cement and sand, taking care that they're correctly proportioned. When you make adjustments, be sure to record them accurately: don't rely on "feel".

Machine-mixing. You can rent, borrow, or buy cement mixers in various sizes, but those under 3 cubic feet in capacity are uneconomical. Set the mixer close to your sand and gravel piles so you can shovel-feed directly. Keep the machine level and chock it in place to prevent "walking".

To mix a small test batch, start the mixer (warm it up first if it's gas-powered) and add a little water. Then add, in order, a little gravel and sand, more water, more gravel and sand, and finally the cement. (Measure your ingredients by shovelfuls as you add them, but be sure not to put the shovel inside the mixer.)

Check the mix by pouring a little out — never look inside a mixer that's running. Mix just until all ingredients are worked in and all particles are wet.

Pouring a Pavement

Whether you're making a single stepping-stone or pouring an entire patio, the basic steps are the same: you'll need to pour and spread the concrete, finish the surface, and then let it cure.

Before you begin, be sure you have enough help for the job. Except in the case of very small projects, concrete work requires at least two people. If you call for a transit-mix truck, you'll certainly need extra hands, especially if you have to move the concrete from one place to another.

Wear rubber boots if you'll have to walk on the concrete. You'll need gloves to protect your hands from concrete's caustic ingredients.

Pouring, spreading, tamping. Start pouring the concrete at one end of the form while a helper uses a shovel or hoe to spread it. Work the concrete up against the form and tamp it into all corners — don't sim-

ply rely on gravity. A splashboard or ramp will save concrete by letting you put it where you want it.

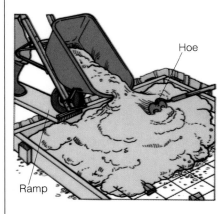

Be sure not to overwork the concrete or spread it too far; overworking will force the heavy aggregate to the bottom of the slab and bring up the "fines"— inert silt that can cause defects in the finished concrete. Instead, space out your pours along the form, working each batch just enough to fill the form completely.

Leveling the concrete. To make the concrete's surface even, you'll need a screed—simply a long, straight board. On long pours, screed batch by batch rather than after all the concrete is placed.

Move the board slowly along the form, using a zigzag, sawing motion. Even on narrow forms, having two people will speed the work and keep it more accurate. A third person can shovel extra concrete into any unfilled pockets.

Floating. Initial floating, done immediately after leveling, smooths down high spots and fills small hollows left after screeding.

If you're using a bull float, as shown below, push it away from you with its leading edge raised slightly and pull it back nearly flat. Overlap your passes.

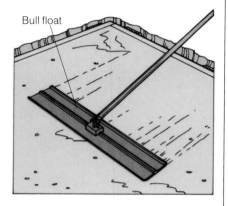

Bull float

Use a darby (see page 18) on smaller projects. Move it in overlapping arcs; then repeat with overlapping straight, side-to-side strokes. Keep the tool flat, but don't let it dig in. On very small projects, a wooden float can be used in a similar manner.

Edging and jointing. The first steps in finishing the floated surface are edging and jointing.

Edging compacts and smooths the area beside the forms, creating a surface resistant to chipping. Begin by running a trowel between the concrete and the form. Follow up with the edger, keeping the forward edge of the tool tilted slightly upward.

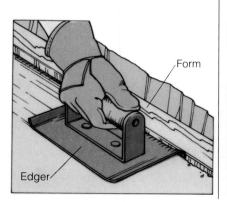

Form
Edger

Jointing induces cracking along a desired course when the concrete expands and contracts during temperature changes. (Permanent dividers serve the same purpose.) Control joints should be made in long walks at intervals no greater than 1½ times the width of the walk; in patio slabs, place them every 10 feet.

Use an edger or a special jointer with a straight board, as shown below, to make control joints. Apply the same pressure and motion as with the edger.

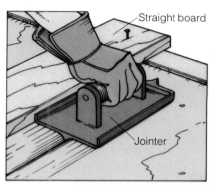

Straight board
Jointer

Final floating and troweling. Unless you want a broomed surface (see below), give the slab a final floating with a wooden float after the water sheen has disappeared from the concrete but before the surface has become really stiff. Kneel on boards to reach the center of a large slab.

For a smoother surface, follow with a steel trowel. Make your initial passes with the trowel flat on the surface; use some pressure, but don't let the blade dig in.

Steel trowel

Creating a nonskid surface. For a nonskid surface, substitute brooming for final floating and troweling. Drag the broom over the concrete after edging and jointing, always pulling it toward you. Avoid overlapping passes, which tend to knock down the grain texture and produce crumbs. Finish up by redoing the edges.

Avoid overlap

Curing. Hydration—a process whereby cement and water combine chemically—is the key to hardness in finished concrete.

You cure concrete by keeping it wet. To do this, cover the slab with straw, burlap, or another material that you can wet down as needed. Or cover the surface with plastic sheeting so water evaporating from the concrete will be trapped. If no covering is available, keep the surface damp by frequent hand-sprinkling.

Plastic sheeting

Although the curing process may be complete in just a few days, it's a good idea to let the concrete cure for a week.

CONCRETE **PAVERS**

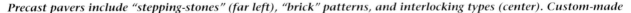

Concrete pavers, in their dozens of clever shapes, have long been used abroad for everything from patios to roadways. Now made in this country, pavers are being used increasingly in residential work. Precast pavers are an ideal material for do-it-yourselfers. A weekend or two of work laying pavers—a relatively inexpensive project—can result in a dramatic patio or garden walkway.

Available in many sizes, colors, and textures, pavers are no longer limited to the 12-inch squares you've seen for years. Shapes include circles, rectangles, and puzzle-piece contours that interlock. Paver selection may vary with location.

A simple square can be part of a grid or even a gentle arc. Modern "cobblestone" patterns can butt together to create broad, unbroken surfaces, or they can be spaced apart and surrounded with grass, a ground cover, or gravel for textural interest.

Interlocking pavers are a logical industrial descendant of the old-fashioned, labor-intensive cobblestone. Made of extremely dense concrete pressure-formed in special machines and laid in sand with closed (butted) joints, they form a surface more rigid than bricks. No paver can tip out of alignment without taking several of its neighbors with it; thus, the surface remains intact, even under very substantial loads. Interlocking pavers are available in tan, brown, red, and natural gray, plus blends of these colors.

Modern cobblestone blocks are very popular for casual gardens; butt them tightly together and then sweep sand or soil between the irregular edges.

Turf blocks, a special paver variant, are designed to carry light traffic while retaining and protecting

Precast pavers include "stepping-stones" (far left), "brick" patterns, and interlocking types (center). Custom-made

Elegant interlocking pavers, set in sand, blend smoothly with aggregate steps and shingled planting beds. Invisible edgings, set in mortar or concrete, maintain clean lines while securing field units. Landscape designer: Karen K. Steeb.

pavers (near right) imitate adobe, stone, and Saltillo tiles. Turf block (far right) allows for grassy patios or driveways.

ground-cover plants. These suggest the possibility of grassy patios and driveways, and can build sideyard access routes that stand up to wear.

Concrete "bricks," available in classic red as well as imitation "used" or antique, are increasingly popular as substitutes for the real thing; in many areas, they're significantly less expensive.

Some landscape professionals cast their own pavers in custom shapes, textures, and colors: adobe, stone, and tile replicas are just a few of the options. You can also make your own pavers, though they won't be as strong as standard pressure-formed units.

Paver selection may vary with location. Cost is determined by size and texture; for example, a 12-inch square of 1½-inch-thick concrete seeded with pebbles can cost three times as much as a plain or colored paver of the same size.

Be cautious when choosing colored concrete pavers; the pigment in some is very shallow, and bare concrete may show through deep scratches or chips.

Handsome geometric pattern with gray edging courses is set atop base of filter fabric and packed gravel. Pressure-treated wooden edgings help lock patio in place. Landscape architect: Lankford Associates.

Concrete turf blocks give needed support to this courtyard driveway, while grass-filled openings add welcome greenery.

Symmetrical garden is framed by 12-inch precast pavers, sold at most home centers. The squares were set on compacted soil and spaced 2 inches apart, with gravel between them. Design: Chris Jacobson.

HOW TO LAY PAVERS

Concrete pavers are a practical patio material — durable, relatively inexpensive, and easy to install. And as you can see from the photos on pages 30–33, they come in a variety of shapes and sizes.

Interlocking pavers are laid in sand, just like bricks; alignment is nearly automatic. Regular (noninterlocking) concrete pavers are also used like bricks, but can be set either in sand or dry mortar.

Preparing the Site

Beneath the pavers, you'll need a 1½- to 2-inch-deep base of construction sand—and for colder climates or pavings doubling as driveways, a deeper subbase of crushed gravel and filter fabric (see drawing below). If you must excavate for a path or patio, allow for the thickness of both the pavers and the base. Be sure to provide for adequate drainage and grade (see pages 6–7).

You can let pavers merge with the surrounding landscape, but containing them within edgings (see pages 8–9) will help prevent shifting. Since edgings are installed first, they also serve as good leveling guides for preparing the base and laying the pavers.

Wood and poured concrete are the most popular edging materials for use with concrete pavers. Another possibility is preformed plastic or aluminum edging. Rigid strips are best for a rectangular patio, but they'll also follow curves if kerfed (partially cut) with a hacksaw. Flexible sections handle tight turns. Set preformed edgings below finished paving height.

You'll have less cutting to do if you design a square or rectangular patio whose dimensions allow you to use full pavers. Special edging pieces, available for some interlocking patterns, can eliminate border cutting altogether.

Laying Pavers

Most pavers are heavy and rough. Use a sturdy wheelbarrow to move them, and wear heavy work gloves to protect your hands.

If you have to cut a few pavers, you can probably do the job with a brick set, cutting them the same way as brick (see page 16). But for numerous or complex cuts, rent a tub saw fitted with a diamond blade. To save on the rental fee, lay all the pavers first, positioning and marking the ones to be cut, and setting them aside. Then you can do all the cutting at once (wear safety goggles).

Laying pavers in sand. If your design calls for permanent edgings, prepare the sand bed and lay the pavers as for bricks in sand (see pages 16–17). If you've chosen wood or concrete edgings, use a bladed screed set slightly less than one paver's thickness in depth; for plastic or other recessed edgings, set screed depth at about 1 inch less.

Another method of laying interlocking pavers in sand—with or without edgings — is to set out lengths of PVC pipe (1 to 1½ inches in diameter) several feet apart over a sand bed. Push the pipes into place; add more sand. Then use a straight board (see drawing at top of facing page) to level the sand at the height of the pipes' tops.

PREPARING FOR PAVERS

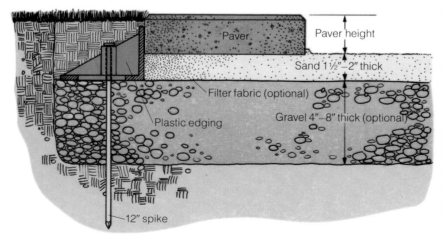

Easy-to-install pavers rest atop bed of packed sand, filter fabric or plastic sheeting, and crushed gravel. Preformed edgings sit below patio surface and are secured by 12-inch spikes.

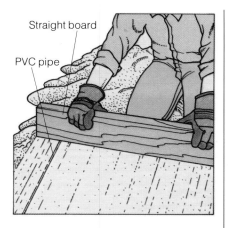

Straight board

PVC pipe

Remove the pipes and smooth over the depressions. Lay the pavers, snugging them into position with a mallet and checking alignment frequently with a level.

Interlocking pavers

Then make several passes with a power plate vibrator to settle them. You can probably rent a vibrator locally; if not, you could substitute a heavy drum roller (see page 56).

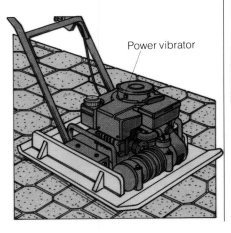

Power vibrator

Finally, spread fine sand over the surface; once it dries, sweep it into paver joints. Additional passes with either vibrator or roller will help lock the pavers together.

Sand

Laying pavers in dry mortar. For a slightly more stable patio with a more formal look than you can get when using only a sand base, consider the dry mortar method (suitable for all except interlocking pavers).

Essentially, you space the units a uniform distance apart (butt them against ⅜-inch plywood, as shown below, to ensure even spacing), and then set and pack them as for pavers laid in sand.

⅜" plywood spacers

Pavers

Instead of sweeping sand into the joints, you add a 1:4 cement-and-sand mortar mix, just as for bricks set in dry mortar (see pages 17–19). Expect some discoloration in the finished patio project.

Casting Your Own Pavers

For a distinctive look that's just right for your needs, consider casting your own concrete blocks in a mold you make yourself.

A simple closed frame made of 2 by 4 lumber is the simplest to construct. For ease in unmolding, hinge two corners, adding a hook and eye to secure the corner. If you need lots of pavers, a multiple-grid form will speed up the job.

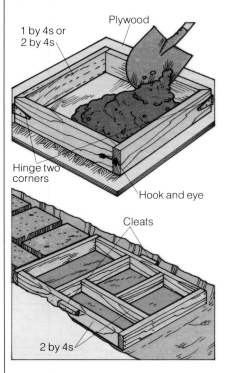

Plywood

1 by 4s or 2 by 4s

Hinge two corners

Hook and eye

Cleats

2 by 4s

Placing a bottom in the box form can lead to all sorts of interesting designs (in this case, the "bottom" of the pour becomes the "top" of the finished block). Moldings, leaves, colored stones, and textured sand are some of the many possibilities.

Oil the form with motor oil or a commercial release agent and place it on a smooth surface. Fill it with a stiff concrete mix, packing in the concrete. Screed with a straight board. You can float the surface if you like, or use the block's smooth underside for the stepping surface. (For concrete specifics, see pages 25–29.)

Let the concrete set for a few hours before unmolding; then cure.

Unglazed terra-cotta and resealed
Saltillo pavers are shown at top;
at top right is slate cut to tile size.
The beige square with individual
"pickets" forms an octagon; man-
made stone tiles are at lower right.
Colorful hand-painted tiles work
well as accents—they're too slick
for overall paving.

CERAMIC **TILE**

Tile works well in both formal and informal garden situations. Its earthy brown and red tones blend with natural colors outdoors, and the hand-fired pigments are permanent and nonfading. Because tile looks great indoors too, it's a good flooring choice for an indoor room that relates to a patio as well as for the patio itself.

Tile paving does have some drawbacks, however. It's costly compared to brick—two to three times as much per square foot. Also, the smooth, slick surface of some types can give off harsh reflections and become slippery when wet—a hazard around a swimming pool or spa.

Glazed or Unglazed?

Glaze is a hard finish, usually colored, applied to the clay surface before final baking. Most bright, flashy tiles you see in tile display rooms are glazed.

Unless a special grit is added to glazed tiles, they can make treacherous footing when wet. The solution? Opt for unglazed tiles for paving, reserving the colorful glazed tiles for occasional accents or for edgings or raised planting beds.

Tile Types

Most outdoor tile falls into one of three categories: pavers, quarry tile, or synthetic stone.

Pavers are made by pouring the clay into wooden or metal molds, removing the molds, drying or curing the tiles, and then firing them. They usually have a grainy, handcrafted look. Perhaps the best-known hand-molded pavers are Saltillo tiles (named for the city in Mexico where they are made). It's not wise to use pavers outdoors in cool, wet climates, where mildew and moss are likely to become problems.

Quarry tiles are denser and more regular in shape than pavers. They come glazed or unglazed, in natural shades of yellow, brown, and red. These tiles are made by squeezing

Dining veranda and patio employ square tiles in several sizes; brick stair trim and edgings provide soft highlights. Landscape architect: Robert W. Chittock & Associates.

French paver squares are hand-rubbed with penetrating stain, set off by dark grout lines. New "used" brick stairs and planters serve as accents. Landscape architect: Delaney & Cochran.

Ceramic Tile   **37**

clay into forms under great pressure, then firing them until they're quite hard. They're available with rounded edges and in corrugated finishes.

Synthetic stone is now being developed by tile manufacturers spurred by the increasing popularity of stone. These tiles, which mimic the look of granite and sandstone, generally have enough surface bite to be used on patios. Colors include black and various shades of gray and beige.

To Seal or Not to Seal?

Some unglazed tiles are sealed at the factory; unsealed, unglazed units should be sealed with a penetrating sealer (which allows the tile to "breathe") after installation.

A sealer may darken the tile's surface or give it a shiny appearance, so you may wish to test it first. Ask your tile dealer to recommend the sealer most appropriate for your situation.

There's no law against having fun with tile! These lizard details were fashioned from tile shards set in mortared background.

Cleaned and resealed with a penetrating sealer, mildewed Mexican pavers regained their tawny, yellow-orange color. Octagonal field tiles join on four edges; small squares complete the pattern.

Saltillo tile stepping pads that link home and outdoor living areas match the inside floors of the house, tying home and garden together. Landscape designer: Jodie Collins.

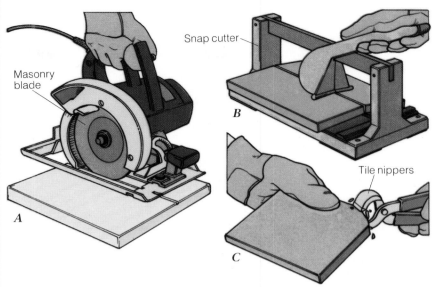

A tub saw with a diamond blade is the best device for cutting tiles, but a circular saw and masonry blade (A) or a snap cutter (B) will work, too. Nibble curves with tile nippers (C).

HOW TO LAY TILE

L aying tile is well within the capabilities of the home mason, but it cannot be a rush job. Because tiles are such precise building units, the slightest flaws in installation may be noticeable. The work must be thoughtfully planned in advance.

Grade the site very carefully (see pages 6–7); an uneven base may cause cracking later. Depending on the tile you choose, you can set the units in sand or in mortar. If you're using mortar, take care not to stain the tiles with it.

Layout Pointers

Carefully measure the area to be covered. Then calculate the number of tiles you need to buy according to the size you've chosen. (Unless you're butting tiles in a sand bed, be sure to allow for ½-inch mortar joints; see page 41). Most pros order 10 to 15 percent extra to allow for cuts and breakage. Mix tiles from box to box as you work to ensure a consistent appearance.

If you must cut a lot of tiles, it's easiest to mark the cutting lines and have the cuts done at a masonry yard equipped with a diamond-bladed saw. For do-it-yourself cutting, a rented tub saw (see page 34) is best; but if you have only a few cuts, a portable circular saw with a masonry-cutting blade, or a snap cutter (which can be rented from a tile dealer) will also do the job. Use tile nippers (shown above) for irregular shapes.

Laying Tile in Sand

Tiles that are at least ¾ inch thick can be laid in sand. Level the soil to allow for a ½-inch-deep sand bed plus the thickness of the tile. (If you make the bed more than ½ inch deep, the tiles may tilt when stepped on.)

Build permanent edgings (see pages 8–9) to hold the tiles in place, setting the edgings so their tops will be flush with the finished surface.

Then lay a bed of damp sand, leveling it with a bladed screed (shown below) drawn along the edgings. Screed about 3 feet at a time, moving any temporary guides along with you.

For a firm base, tamp the sand, add more, and screed again. One cubic foot of sand will cover about 20 square feet to a depth of ½ inch.

For extra stability, you can add dry cement to the setting bed—1 part cement to each 8 parts sand. Before mixing, sift the cement through household screening.

Lay tiles with either open joints (½ inch for small tiles, ¾ inch for larger ones) or closed joints (provided sizes are uniform).

Starting at a corner, set the tiles in place, tapping with a rubber mallet to bed them in the sand. Check for level as you go.

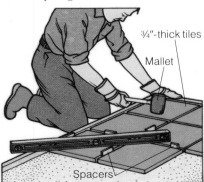

Adobe:
A Touch of the Old Southwest

Few materials can give a quality of rustic ease to a garden the way adobe does. Spaced with 1-inch open joints, adobe creates a living floor; low-growing plants and moss fill the joints, softening the look (and feel) of the area paved.

Rugged adobe walls also add color, texture, and—due to their thickness—coolness to an enclosed patio. The most common block size is 4 by 7½ by 16 inches, about the same as four or five clay bricks put together.

Historically, adobe structures were doomed to decay, victims of the combined forces of summer heat and winter rain. Today, however, adobe is made with an asphalt stabilizer that keeps the bricks from dissolving.

Although adobe is most commonly found in the southwestern U.S., it can be used effectively almost anywhere in the country. Check prices with local building supply dealers, however, because delivery charges can make it somewhat costly.

Paving pointers

Laying adobe in sand allows for good drainage and extends the life of the blocks. Use a 2-inch sand bed, but be sure it's completely level. If you allow blocks to straddle humps or bridge hollows, they may break.

Adobe blocks for walks and walls (above) come in a variety of sizes and shapes, depending on local sources. In stepped walkway (right), adobe complements rugged look of railroad ties. The ties hold blocks in place; sand bed fills the spaces. Landscape contractor: Grimes Natural Landscapes, Inc.

Because the dimensions of adobe blocks vary slightly, it's usually difficult to lay them in patterns that call for tight fitting. Leave 1-inch open joints between units and scoop out or fill in sand as necessary to compensate for irregularities.

Running bond, jack-on-jack, and basket-weave patterns (see page 15) all work well, and the latter two require no cutting. If you do need to cut adobe, however, it's easy to do with a sledge and brick set (see page 16) or with an old saw.

Fill the joints with sand or soil. Filling with soil permits crevice planting, which gives a softer look.

Wall-building tips

The method for constructing an adobe wall is similar to that used in laying bricks (pages 71–73). But adobe is considerably more cumbersome to handle: the blocks weigh up to 45 pounds apiece.

Because of their weight, adobe walls require a sturdy foundation (see pages 64–66). You can add tensile strength by using steel reinforcing rods (consult your building department for specific requirements). Reinforcement is also required at the corners.

For adobe wall construction, you'll need a mortar mixture that's leaner than for bricks. Use 1 part cement, 2 parts soil (the same as in the bricks), 3 parts sand, and 1¼ gallons of stabilizer per sack of cement (about 1 part per shovelful). If you like, you can paint the adobe to match its surroundings; latex works well.

Spread sand over the surface. After it dries, sweep it into the joints, filling all of them. Finally, wet the area with a fine spray, adding more sand as required.

Laying Tile in Wet Mortar

Shown below is a particularly stable method of laying tile—in a 1-inch mortar bed over an existing concrete slab or a newly poured one (for basic concrete techniques, see pages 25-29). If using an old slab, wash it with a diluted muriatic acid solution and rinse well. Then brush a coat of cement-and-water paste over the surface.

You can also tile over a wooden deck, porch, or stairway, provided the structure can support the added weight without flexing. Nail a layer of waterproof building paper over the flooring. Then stretch out a reinforcing mesh of ¾-inch chicken wire and nail it down, leaving ¼ inch between the wire and the surface.

Install permanent or temporary edgings; they should rise above the base a height equal to the thickness of the tile plus the 1-inch thickness of the mortar bed. Lay a stiff (1:4) cement-sand mortar bed atop the concrete, leveling it with a bladed screed. Pour the mortar in batches of 20 square feet or less.

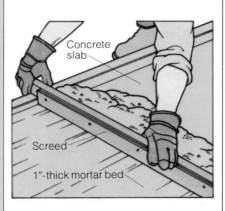

Then lay the tiles, leaving ½-inch open joints (use pieces of plywood for spacers and mason's line for alignment). Tap the centers of the tiles with a rubber mallet, and check fre-

quently with a level. Let the mortar set for 24 hours.

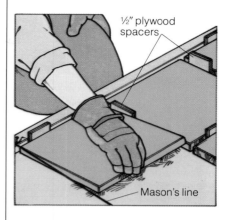

Prepare a 1:3 cement-sand mixture to use as grout for the joints; it should be just thin enough to pour. Use a bent can to fill the joints, removing any smudges or spills immediately with a damp sponge.

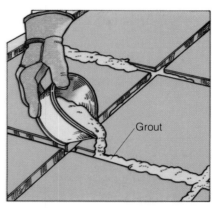

When the grout begins to harden, tool the joints as shown. Keep the mortar damp for the first day. Stay off the paved area for 3 days.

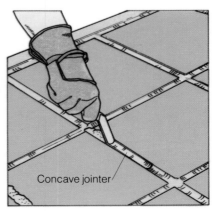

STONE PAVING

Square stone tiles, fashioned from Idaho quartzite, make an elegant veranda floor. Stone is set in mortar atop a rigid slab; grout lines were kept impeccably thin. Landscape architect: The Berger Partnership, P.S.

Stone pavings have the appeal of a thoroughly natural material, and most are very durable. Flat flagstones and cut stone are ideal for formal paving. For a more informal look, you can use more irregularly shaped rocks and pebbles, setting them on soil or embedding them in concrete.

Marble and granite are igneous (volcanic) rock, and create the hardest surfaces. Sandstone, limestone, and other sedimentary stones are more porous; they usually have a chalky or gritty texture. Dense, smooth slate is a fine-grained metamorphic rock. The availability of

You'll find a good selection of random-

A traditional cobblestone paving lends a comfortable feel to this detached garden patio. The stones must be laid in firm soil or sand; soil and plantings fill the spaces between units.

size flagstones at most garden centers. We show ones most often used, but offerings vary by region—and by supplier.

stone types, shapes, sizes, and colors varies by locale.

Stone's primary drawback is that it can cost up to five times as much as brick or concrete. Geography dictates cost: the farther you are from the quarry, the more you'll have to pay.

Flagstone

Technically, flagstone is any flat stone that's either naturally thin or split from rock that cleaves easily. Flagstone works well in almost any garden setting. Its casual look blends well with plants, and it's one of the few paving materials that can be set directly on stable soil.

Flagstone does have its drawbacks. It's costly. Because of its irregularity, it's not a good surface for outdoor furniture, games, or wheeled playthings. Some types of flagstone soil easily and are difficult to clean (ask your supplier about the characteristics of the specific stone you're considering). And flagstone must be laid out very carefully, or you can end up with an awkward-looking patchwork.

Stone Tiles

Many stone types are available precut in rectangular shapes. Some have random widths and thicknesses. Granite and slate, which come in many colors, are popular—but expensive.

Stone tiles are usually laid with very thin grout lines, which gives them a more formal look.

Other Stones

Fieldstones, river rocks, and pebbles are less expensive than flagstone.

The paving pattern makes this straight walkway a distinctive side yard. One-foot squares of lilac Pennsylvania stone, laid diagonally, are bordered by 9-by-18-inch stones. Landscape architect: René Fransen.

A new flagstone patio and pool deck uses individual stones in tones of gray, green, and brown that complement the mottled tones of the existing brick walls of the house. A drain hidden beneath gray river stones keeps runoff from the planting beds out of the pool, so the water stays cleaner. Architect: Dale Selzer. Landscape architect: Naud Burnett.

These water-worn or glacier-ground stones produce rustic, uneven pavings that make up in charm for what they may lack in smoothness underfoot.

River rocks and pebbles are available in countless shapes and sizes, are impervious to weather, and are virtually maintenance-free. Smaller stones and pebbles can be set or seeded into concrete; large stones can be laid directly on soil as raised stepping-stones. An entire surface can be paved solid with cobblestones set in concrete or tamped earth. Or use narrow mosaic panels to break up an expanse of concrete or brick.

There are some negatives to consider. Some natural stones are very smooth and can become dangerously slick in wet weather. Because their shapes are irregular, they may be uncomfortable to walk on; this is especially true of rounded cobblestones. Laying a pavement of natural stone is a very slow process, particularly when you're working with small pebbles and stones in mortar or concrete. It's best to confine such surfacing to a limited area.

Every garden needs a seating area. Here an arbor covered with crossvine shades a limestone terrace. Compacted, decomposed granite gives the adjacent courtyard a natural look. Architect: Ted Flato. Landscape architect: Rosa Finsley.

HOW TO LAY STONE

I rregularly shaped flagstones can be set in firm soil, in a sand bed, or in mortar (atop a concrete base). Tighter-fitting precut rectangles work well laid in a bed of sand.

River rocks and fieldstones are rustic alternatives to flagstone. Depending on the size of the stones, you can seed them into concrete or place them individually in mortar or in a concrete setting bed.

Working with Flagstone

Since most flagstones are irregularly shaped, you'll probably need to fit and cut pieces before setting them. After preparing the area (see pages 6–7) and adding edgings (see pages 8–9) if appropriate, lay out the flagstones, shifting them around until you achieve a pleasing design that requires a minimum of cutting.

When a stone needs shaping, let the adjoining one overlap it. Mark the cutting line with a pencil, using the edge of the top stone as a guide.

Score a $\frac{1}{8}$-inch-deep groove along the cutting line with a brick set or, for greater accuracy, a portable circular saw fitted with a masonry blade. Place a length of wood or metal pipe under the stone so that the waste portion and the scored line overhang it. Strike sharply along the line with a brick set and sledge (wear safety glasses).

For smaller trimming jobs, chip off pieces with a mason's hammer or a sharp brick set.

Laying Stones in Sand

Stones laid in a bed of sand provide a stable patio surface, especially when shapes are uniform. The sand helps lock units together. You use the same technique as for laying bricks in sand (see pages 16–17).

Place rectangular stones in a tight pattern, bedding each unit with a mallet and checking with a level (see drawing below). Scoop out or fill in sand to compensate for variations in the thickness of the stone.

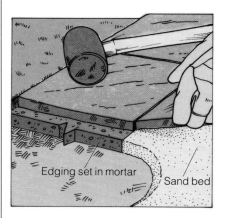

Edging set in mortar   Sand bed

If you're using irregularly shaped flagstones, the stones should be firmly bedded over their entire surface so they won't wobble when walked on. Pack the joints with soil.

Laying Flagstones in Wet Mortar

To achieve the most permanent flagstone surface possible, set stones in a mortar bed over at least a 3-inch-thick concrete slab, either existing (clean and in good condition) or new (see pages 25–29). Ask your concrete dealer whether you need to use a bonding agent on the slab's surface. If the stones are porous, wet them a few hours before setting them.

Setting stones. Before laying the mortar bed, arrange the stones, cutting and trimming them so there's a minimum of space for mortar joints.

Prepare a 1:3 cement-sand mixture, enough to cover 10 to 12 square feet, adding water slowly. The mortar should be stiff enough to support the weight of the stones, but not so stiff that you can't work it.

FITTING & CUTTING FLAGSTONE

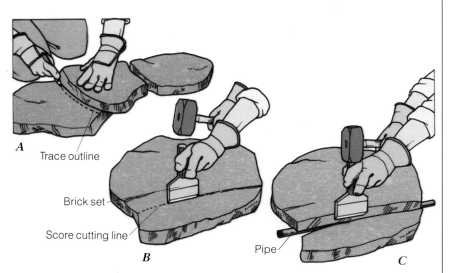

A Trace outline

Brick set

Score cutting line

B

Pipe

C

To custom-fit irregular flagstone, lay one block over its neighbor and trace its outline (A). Then score a $\frac{1}{8}$-inch groove in stone to be cut (B). Finally, prop up stone and split with a sharp blow (C).

Starting at one corner, remove a manageable section of stones and set them aside. With a trowel, spread enough mortar (at least 1 inch deep for the thickest stones) to make a full bed for one or two stones. Furrow the mortar with your trowel.

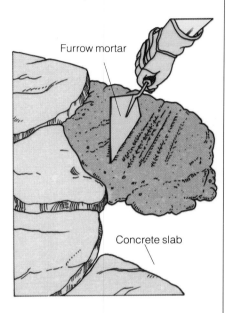
Furrow mortar

Concrete slab

Set each stone firmly in place, bedding it with a rubber mallet.

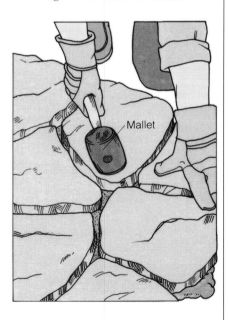
Mallet

To maintain an even surface, use a straightedge and a level. Clean the stones with a damp sponge as you work.

Grouting joints. When the mortar has set for 24 hours, pack the joints with the same mortar mix used for the bed—plus an optional ½ to 1 part fireclay to improve workability—and smooth them with a trowel or jointer. Clean the stones as you work.

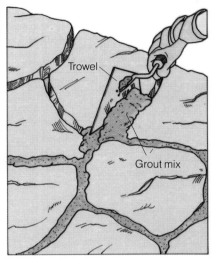
Trowel

Grout mix

Keep the grout damp for the first day by sprinkling it with water or by covering it with plastic sheeting. Keep off the paved area for 3 days.

Laying Pebbles or Cobbles

Flattened stones 6 inches or more in diameter can be set directly in soil for a natural look. Smaller cobbles, river stones, or pebbles should be set in mortar or seeded into concrete. The latter method requires wood forms.

Setting mosaics in mortar. You can set decorative pebbles on an existing slab that's clean and in good condition or on a new one. Leave the surface rough and let the concrete cure for at least 24 hours.

Prepare a 1:3 cement-sand mortar mixture and spread it over the slab to a depth of ½ inch. Stones should be set in the mortar within 2 hours, so spread only as much mortar as you can fill within that time; cut dry edges away from the previous mortar bed before spreading the current section. Keep stones in a pail of clean water, setting them in the mortar while they're still wet.

Mortar bed   River stones

Push stones in deep enough so the mortar gets a good hold on their edges—generally, just past the middle. Use a board to keep the stones level.

Straight board

Let the mortar set for 2 to 3 hours; then spread another thin layer of mortar over the surface and into the voids. Hose and brush away any excess mortar before it sets.

Setting stones in wet concrete. To seed tiny pebbles, build forms, pour the concrete, and level the surface; then follow the instructions for seeding aggregates on page 26.

For larger stones, pour the slab as above, but don't fill the forms completely. Push the stones into the concrete one by one, sinking slightly more than half the stone. When the concrete has hardened somewhat, expose the stones by brushing the concrete while wetting down the surface with a fine spray.

WOOD PAVING

Few materials can match the natural, informal quality of wood. Its warm color and soft texture bring something of the forest into your garden. And because wood blends well with other paving materials, it works gracefully in transition zones between masonry patio areas.

Rounds, Blocks & Ties

Wood may be used as unit paving in several ways: round disks can be em-bedded in random patterns in sand over gravel; square blocks can be laid like bricks; railroad ties or timbers can be combined with other paving materials to build a bold-looking, durable surface.

Wood rounds or blocks, often set in place with the end grain in contact with the soil, soak up ground moisture; the wood eventually rots.

For this reason, it's best to choose rot- and insect-resistant heartwood of

Low-level cedar deck floats above rock garden and bridges garden pool; 2 by 3 decking boards are finished with semitransparent stain. Matching benches float atop pressure-treated posts. Landscape architect: Lankford Associates.

Wood   **49**

cedar, redwood, or cypress. Or use lumber pressure-treated with preservatives. Look for wood that's specifically prepared for ground contact and stamped as such. Specify lumber with a retention level of 0.40; "retention" refers to the amount of preservative in the wood. (The pressure-treated wood typically used for above-ground decking has a retention level of 0.25 and is not recommended for in-ground construction.)

Railroad ties, pretreated against rot and insect damage, will last for many years. Standard ties measure 6 inches by 8 inches by 8 feet and weigh anywhere from 100 to 140 pounds each. In some areas, shorter lengths are also available.

Low-level Decks

Other good uses for wood outdoors include low-level decks (which can bridge uneven spots or extend a flat patio past a drop in grade) and raised pathways and steps.

Deck lumber is durable and resilient underfoot, and does not store heat the way other surfacing materials can. In addition, its light weight (2 to 12 pounds per square foot) makes installation very convenient for the do-it-yourselfer. And because it's available in a wide variety of species, grades, and sizes, wood adapts easily to individual budgets and architectural styles. Depending on the effect you desire, you can let your deck weather naturally or you can paint, stain, or oil it.

Wooden decks do need periodic maintenance. You may need to remove mildew or fungus, rust stains from nails, and splinters; or the finish may require a touch-up. Unlike other outdoor surfacing materials, wood is vulnerable to fire and termites.

Wood rounds march down a casual, overgrown path; spaces between blend with surroundings. Be sure to choose lumber that's resistant to moisture decay and insects.

Deck module tilts into position during installation. Parallel 1 by 4 cleats on underside hold decking boards together. Deck supports are 2 by 6s; they radiate from central 4 by 4 posts anchored to movable concrete piers. Landscape architect: Katherine and Steve Evans.

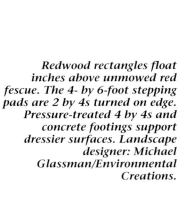

Redwood rectangles float inches above unmowed red fescue. The 4- by 6-foot stepping pads are 2 by 4s turned on edge. Pressure-treated 4 by 4s and concrete footings support dressier surfaces. Landscape designer: Michael Glassman/Environmental Creations.

HOW TO BUILD WITH WOOD

Wood rounds, blocks, and timbers are user-friendly materials that give the builder a good deal of freedom in application. But don't expect them to last like masonry, especially in damp or humid climates. Because low-level decking is raised above the ground and can dry quickly, it will survive longer under adverse weather conditions.

Note: Because the primary preservative used in pressure-treated wood contains chromium, a toxic metal, you must wear goggles and a dust mask when cutting it, and you should never burn it.

Preparing the Site

In general, wood paving units require careful site preparation. Grade the area as described on pages 6–7. To protect the wood from excessive ground moisture, put down a layer of filter fabric or plastic sheeting before laying the base or the paving units.

Wood Rounds

Constructing a simple paving made of wood rounds or irregular wood "flagstones" is an easy job.

First, put down a 2-inch-thick bed of sand. Arrange the rounds on top of the sand in a pattern that fills the area and produces a pleasing design. Make sure the tops are flush with the surface of the ground. Then fill the spaces between the rounds with bark, gravel, or large pebbles, or add soil and plant it with grass or a ground cover.

End-grain Blocks

Wood blocks—cross sections sawn from 4 by 4s or larger timbers—can be laid in much the same way as bricks.

When you grade, dig down 1 inch deeper than the thickness of the blocks. Build wood edgings (see pages 8–9), placing the stakes on the outside. Then lay down a 1-inch-thick sand bed. Set the blocks as for bricks in sand (see pages 16–17), then sweep sand into the joints.

This method also works for 1 by 12s or 2 by 12s cut square and laid face up in the sand. Cutting grooves or dadoes down the center of each board with a router or table saw can give the appearance of a basket-weave pattern, as shown below. (However, the groove may hasten decay.)

Railroad Ties

Because they blend well with other patio materials, railroad ties make an effective surface in a limited area. Using them for a large project could prove costly, however.

To set ties flush with the surface, prepare the site as described on pages 6–7. For a raised paving, simply level

EASY WOOD PAVINGS

Wood rounds

2"-thick sand bed

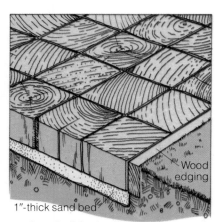
End-grain blocks

1"-thick sand bed

Wood edging

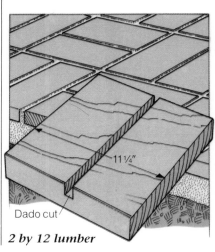
2 by 12 lumber

Dado cut

11¼"

Railroad ties

Gravel

Plastic sheeting

LOW-LEVEL DECK DESIGNS

Sleeper construction

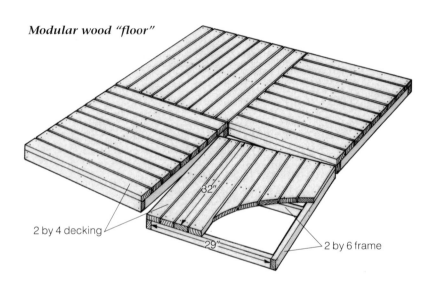

2 by 6 decking

24"

4 by 4 sleeper

Wood shims

Modular wood "floor"

2 by 4 decking

32"

29"

2 by 6 frame

Low-level decking

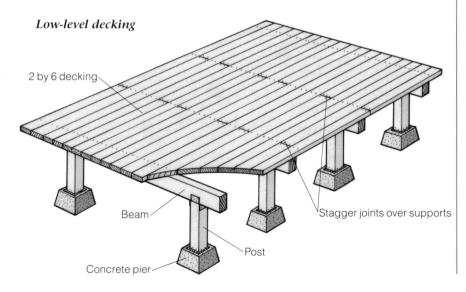

2 by 6 decking

Beam

Concrete pier

Post

Stagger joints over supports

the site and arrange ties directly on the ground. Set the ties on a layer of filter fabric or plastic sheeting or in a sand bed laid over the fabric. Cut ties with a crosscut saw as required.

If you prefer, substitute 6 by 6 pressure-treated timbers for railroad ties, painting or staining them as desired (see facing page).

Sleeper Construction

A raised wooden floor is a handsome, easy-to-build choice where drainage is a problem. Moreover, it adds to the longevity of your patio.

Build a support system, as shown at left, from pressure-treated 4 by 4s laid at 24- to 32-inch intervals; set them on tamped earth or in a bed of sand. Or, if you're decking over an existing slab, substitute 2 by 4 sleepers.

Using galvanized nails or deck screws, attach 2 by 4 or 2 by 6 decking to the supports, centering board ends over supports and staggering the joints between rows.

Modular Decking

Like the sleeper-supported decking described above, modular wood flooring avoids potential drainage problems and has the added benefit of being portable.

Prepare the base as required, then build square or rectangular support frames from 2 by 4s or 2 by 6s; spans between frame members should be 32 inches or less. Using galvanized nails or deck screws, attach 2 by 4 decking, as shown at left. Omit a module here or there to accommodate a boulder or container plant.

Low-level Decks

A low-level deck—either freestanding or house-attached—provides a solid, relatively durable surface requiring little or no grading and a minimum of maintenance. The basic components are shown at left.

For an attached deck, plan to fasten a 2 by 6 ledger to the house siding, at least 2½ inches below any adjacent door opening. Use lag screws for wood siding, or anchor bolts for masonry.

First prop the ledger off the ground with scrap blocks or 2 by 4s and level carefully. Drill pilot holes for two or three fasteners, and secure the ledger in place. Add lag screws or bolts every 16 inches. If your siding is wood, protect the seam with metal flashing, as shown below.

Dig holes no more than 32 inches apart (24 inches is best) for concrete footings, spacing rows about 5 feet apart. Pour the footings and set in precast concrete piers, leveling their tops carefully. Let the concrete cure overnight.

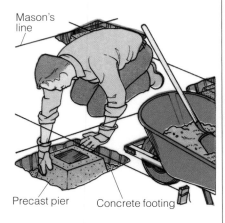

Lay pressure-treated 4 by 4 beams on the piers, adding short posts as necessary to gain the correct height. Level the beams by inserting shingles or shims between the beams and the posts or piers. Secure the beams using framing connectors, as shown, or toenail them to posts or piers. Joints between beams should meet over piers; secure any joints with metal plates or wooden braces.

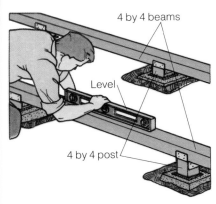

If your deck is attached to the house, connect the beams to the ledger; typically, beams sit in joist hangers nailed to the ledger.

Then add decking boards—flat 2 by 4s, 2 by 6s, varied widths of 2-by lumber, or other sizes laid on edge. Space boards ⅛ to ³⁄₁₆ inch apart to allow for drainage (a 16d nail is a good spacer). An exception: newly pressure-treated Southern (yellow) pine. Butt these boards tightly; they'll shrink as they dry, creating drainage gaps.

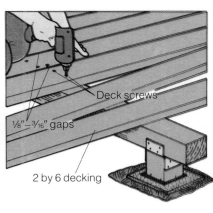

Secure decking with galvanized nails or deck screws. Choose a fastener that's at least twice as long as the deck is thick: for example, 3-inch screws work well for 2 by 6 decking.

You don't need to trim each board flush with the deck's edge. Instead, let them hang over, then cut them all at once, using a portable circular saw. Either snap a chalk line and cut freehand, or clamp on a wooden straightedge to guide the saw's baseplate.

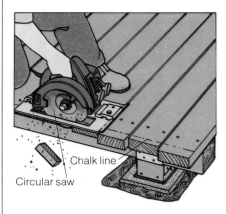

For a more finished appearance, plan to trim the deck edges as shown below. By using 2 by 6 rim joists, you'll be able to neatly cover both the 4 by 4 beams and the ends of the decking boards.

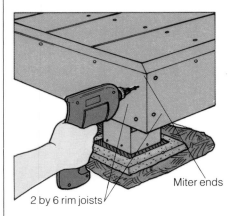

Doing some strategic caulking and applying a clear water repellent, a stain (some come pastel-tinted), or paint can protect your deck and preserve its beauty. Product labels tell you how many coats to apply.

Generally, it's best to paint or stain decking as soon as it's laid. However, let newly pressure-treated or very green (wet) lumber dry about two months before finishing.

LOOSE MATERIALS

Hardwood bark is a natural choice for a garden path. For drainage and stability, lay bark or chips over a compacted base.

Loose materials come by the sack or the truckload. From top to bottom are shredded bark, redwood chips, decomposed granite, quartz pebbles, redrock, river rocks.

For economy, good drainage, and a more casual look, consider including such materials as pea gravel, bark, or wood chips in your patio plan.

You needn't opt for the large, uninteresting expanses that give some aggregates a bad name. Gravel can be raked into patterns or used as a decorative element with other paving materials. You can set off different gravel types with dividers. You can combine gravel or wood chips with concrete pads, concrete pavers, or other stepping-stones. Gravel or other loose materials can also be used effectively in transition zones between patio and garden; they tend to complement plants attractively.

Wood Chips and Bark

By-products of lumber mills, wood chips and shredded bark are springy and soft underfoot, generally inexpensive, and easy to apply. You'll probably find a wide variety of colors and textures. To work successfully as patio surfaces, they should be confined inside a grid with headers.

Wood chips make a good cushion under swings and slides in children's play areas.

Shredded bark, sometimes called gorilla hair, is the most casual of the loose materials. It compacts well and is useful as a transitional material between plantings.

Rock

Gravel is collected or mined from natural deposits. Crushed rock is mechanically fractured and then graded to a uniform size. If the surface of the rock has been naturally worn smooth by water, it's called river rock. Frequently, gravels are named after the regions where they were quarried.

When making a choice, consider color, sheen, texture, and size. Take home samples as you would paint chips. Keep in mind that gravel color, like paint color, looks more intense when spread over a large area.

Low-maintenance pathway of pea gravel fills in between raised wood beds and complements rustic wood wall.

Tan gravel chips form a backdrop for poetic placement of flagstone and small garden pool. Gray-blue pea gravel winds in stream fashion through the scene.

LAYING DOWN LOOSE MATERIALS

Pea gravel, shredded bark, pecan shells, redrock: these are just a few of the loose materials, or aggregates, available for pavings. They blend well with concrete pavers and pads, wood rounds and decking modules, or native stones and boulders. All are sold by the sack, by the cubic yard, and by the ton.

Preparing the Site

Unless compacted, loose materials are easily scattered and difficult to walk on. And if you don't use filter fabric or heavy plastic sheeting underneath them, weeds may poke through. These materials stand up best when spread over a more permanent bed of pea gravel or decomposed granite.

To begin, prepare the area to be paved (see pages 6–7), taking into account the recommended depth for the material you're using. Then install wood or masonry edgings (see pages 8–9) to hold the loose material in bounds. For a large area, consider using a grid of 2 by 4 dividers (built the same way as wood edgings) to help keep the paving material more uniformly distributed.

Place sheets of filter fabric or polyethylene plastic on the ground before laying the paving. The liner provides effective bedding and discourages the growth of weeds. Puncture plastic every square foot or so to allow for drainage.

Gravel

Gravel—either smooth river rock or more angular crushed material—makes a low-cost, fast-draining surface. It's particularly effective when used in low-traffic areas or in combination with smoother, tougher masonry units or poured concrete. Coverage varies with size and weight, but generally, you'll need one ton of rock to cover 100 square feet.

Gravel surfaces tend to shift when walked on, but this can be minimized by using a compacted base of crushed rock or sand.

You'll need a wheelbarrow and an iron rake for hauling and spreading and a large drum roller (available at rental centers) to pack both the base and the gravel.

Laying the base. After installing edgings, put down filter fabric or plastic sheeting for weed protection. Then lay down decomposed granite or sand over the site, taking care not to disturb the liner.

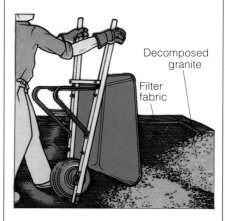
Decomposed granite / Filter fabric

Rake out the base material evenly over the site, forming a uniform

1-inch thickness. As you rake, wet the granite or sand with a fine spray.

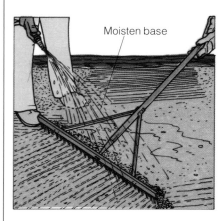
Moisten base

Using a drum roller, roll the wet base several times to pack it evenly. A firm base helps keep the gravel topcoat from shifting underfoot.

Drum roller

Adding gravel. Finally, spread the gravel topcoat 2 to 3 inches thick and rake it evenly over the base.

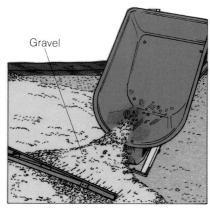
Gravel

Using the drum roller, press the topcoat into place (the rolling will also help turn sharp edges down).

Adding stepping-stones. An excellent way to make a gravel patio more stable is to add stepping-stones—either thick flagstones or concrete pavers. Place the stepping-stones on packed base material so that their tops protrude slightly above the surrounding gravel.

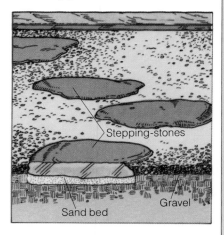

Wood Chips & Bark

Chips and bark, by-products of the lumber industry, are available in a variety of sizes and colors.

Lay redwood or pine bark 2 to 4 inches thick on the prepared base. Shredded bark (redwood or cypress) or pine straw make springy, natural-looking top dressings over a wood-chip base. Or use them atop decomposed granite or crushed rock.

Decomposed Granite & Crushed Rock

Because particle size ranges from sand to quite large pieces of rock, decomposed granite and crushed rock make good pavings that pack tightly together and don't move underfoot.

Lay these materials over the prepared site the same way you would a decomposed granite base for gravel (see facing page). In this case, however, plan to build up a 2½- to 4-inch-thick paving in 1-inch increments.

Asphalt Answers

What can you do with an old asphalt driveway or walk that's seen better days? You can either give it a face-lift, or remove all or part of it in favor of new paving or plantings. Here's a quick course in the basics.

Dress it up. To patch small potholes, buy ready-to-use loose asphalt. Pour it out, rake it even, then pack it down, following the manufacturer's instructions. For deep fissures, apply a concentrated filler before spreading with a top coating (see below).

To seal old asphalt, you'll need either basic coating or a slightly thicker coating-plus-filler. Oil-emulsion coating, though hard to find, is the choice of many professionals. Better grades dry in a few days and hold up better than coal-tar products.

Tear it out. If you need to remove asphalt, you could rent a pike (pry bar) or jackhammer—just be sure you're ready for a vigorous workout.

On a cool day, a large pike can enable you to pry up 1-foot-square asphalt chunks nearly as fast as with a small jackhammer. On a hot day, however, it's a different story. Warmed to the consistency of tar, asphalt bends when it's pried, and sticks to everything in sight.

The lightest pneumatic jackhammer, a 30-pounder, is suited for breaking asphalt 2 to 3 inches thick. Electric jackhammers are even smaller, lighter, and quieter. They're also less powerful, but can handle relatively thin paving. Whichever model you choose, you'll need a wide asphalt-removing blade to go with it.

Concrete pavers, timber edgings, and gravel border give a new lift to an existing asphalt driveway. Landscape architect: Lankford Associates.

Large native stones lead from the side yard to a terrace. The stones rise unevenly, a deliberate ploy to make you slow down and appreciate the quiet interplay of shade-loving plants. Garden designers: Tom Mannion and Louise Kane.

GARDEN **STEPS**

Garden steps can be gracious accents that set the mood for an entire landscaping scheme.

Most inviting are wide, deep steps that lead the eye to a garden focal point; such steps can also serve as a retaining wall, create a base for a planter, or provide additional seating. To soften the edges of a series of steps, as well as to help mark them for walkers, place containers, plantings, or open beds along their borders.

Poured concrete and masonry block units usually present a formal, substantial look. Natural materials such as stone and wood add an informal touch and appear at home in a less structured garden scheme. (In addition, less formal steps are usually simpler to build.)

Constructing steps of the same material used in the patio or for garden walls helps unite an overall landscape design. Using contrasting materials draws attention to the steps and the parts of the garden they serve. Combining materials can effect a transition between unlike surfaces. For example, you can link a brick patio to a concrete walk by building steps made of concrete treads and brick risers.

Regardless of the material you use, put safety first: treads must give safe footing in wet weather, and adequate lighting should be provided.

Peeled-log risers complement a Japanesque garden scheme. Smaller log stakes secure them; gravel fill is held in check by curved benderboard.

How do you integrate a set of aggregate stairs into the garden? Widen them to form a landing, then soften with ground covers and border plantings. The result is a graceful series of terraces. Landscape architect: Robert W. Chittock & Associates.

STEP-BUILDING BASICS

Well-designed steps begin with an understanding of proper proportions. Concrete (embedded with masonry units, if desired), railroad ties, and dimension lumber are all appropriate materials.

Design Principles

To design steps, you must first determine the proportions of the steps and the degree of the slope.

Proportions. The flat part of a step is called the tread; the vertical element is the riser. Ideally, the depth of the tread plus twice the riser height equals 25 to 27 inches. The ideal step has a 6-inch-high riser and a 15-inch-deep tread. As the chart below shows, riser and tread dimensions can vary, but the overall riser-tread relationship should remain the same.

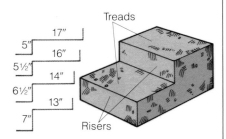

Treads

5"   17"
5½"   16"
6½"   14"
7"   13"

Risers

15"
6"

Ideal tread/riser relationship

Risers should be no lower than 5 inches and no higher than 8 inches. Tread depth should never be less than 11 inches. And all the risers and treads in any one flight of steps should be uniform in size.

Dimensions. Using the drawing below as a guide, calculate the distance from A to B; this is the rise, or change in level, of your slope. The distance from A to C is the run, the minimum length your steps will run.

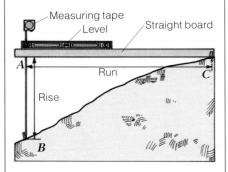

Measuring tape
Level
Straight board
A
Run
C
Rise
B

To determine the number of steps you'll need, divide the desired riser height into the total rise of the slope. If the answer ends in a fraction (and it probably will), drop the fraction and divide the whole number into the vertical distance; the resulting figure will give you the exact measurement for each of your risers. Check the chart to see if the corresponding minimum tread will fit into the slope's total run.

Plan on a minimum width of 2 feet for simple utility steps. For other steps, 4 feet is a good minimum width—5 feet if you want two people to be able to walk abreast.

Fitting the terrain. Rarely will the steps fit exactly into a slope as it is. Plan to cut and fill the slope, as shown on page 92, to accommodate the steps.

If your slope is too steep even for 8-inch risers, remember that steps need not run straight up and down. Curves and switchbacks make the walking distance longer, but the climb gentler.

Masonry Steps

Steps can be built entirely of concrete, or the concrete can be used as a base for mortared masonry units.

Preparing the base and building forms. First, form rough steps in the earth, keeping the treads as level and the risers as perpendicular as possible. Allow space for at least a 6-inch gravel setting bed and a 4-inch thickness of concrete on both treads and risers. (In severe climates, you may need 6 to 8 inches of concrete, plus a footing that's sunk below the frost line.) If you're adding masonry units, add these thicknesses to tread and/or riser dimensions. Tamp any filled areas thoroughly, substituting coarse (¾-inch or larger) aggregate for earth where possible.

Using 2-inch-thick lumber, build forms similar to the wood edgings described on pages 8–9.

Lay the gravel bed, keeping it 4 inches back from the front of the steps; this way, the concrete will be extra-thick at that potentially weak point. To reinforce, add 6-inch-square welded mesh as for concrete paving.

Pouring and finishing. Pour and screed the concrete as for a poured concrete paving. For more weather-safe treads, broom the surfaces to roughen them. Cure as for paving.

If your plans call for installing bricks, pavers, or other masonry units over the concrete, follow the steps for patio pavings of the chosen material.

Railroad-tie Steps

Railroad ties make simple but rugged steps. Installation is relatively easy, but because ties are quite heavy, you'll almost certainly need a helper.

Excavate the site, tamping the soil in the tread area very firmly.

On firm soil, the ties can be secured with ½-inch galvanized steel pipes or ¾-inch reinforcing rods. Drill a hole about 12 inches in from each end of each tie. Then, using a sledge, drive the pipes or rods through these holes directly into the ground.

For extra support, pour small concrete footings. Set anchor bolts in the slightly stiffened concrete. When the concrete has set (after about 2 days), bolt the ties to the footings.

Once the ties are in place, fill the tread spaces behind them with concrete, brick-in-sand paving, or another material of your choice.

If you prefer, substitute 6 by 6 pressure-treated timbers for railroad ties. Semitransparent stain or enamel can tame the greenish cast of chemical-treated wood. It's best to wait a few months before finishing.

Wooden Steps

Formal wooden steps are best for a low-level deck or for easy access from a house. Two of the most common types of straight-run wood steps are shown at right. Steps with treads supported by wood or metal cleats are easier to build than those with treads cut into stringers.

Make stringers from 2 by 10s or 2 by 12s. (If the steps are more than 4 feet wide, you'll need a third stringer in the middle.)

Use galvanized bolts or metal joist hangers to secure the stringers to a deck beam or joist; if you're running stringers off stucco siding or another masonry surface, hang them on a ledger, as shown at right. Note that when bolts are used, the first tread is below the surface of the interior floor or deck; with joist hangers, the first tread must be level with the floor.

Secure the stringers at the bottom to wood nailing blocks anchored in a concrete footing.

If you're planning just one or two steps, consider box construction. Simply assemble individual frames for each level, add treads, then stack and secure each box as shown.

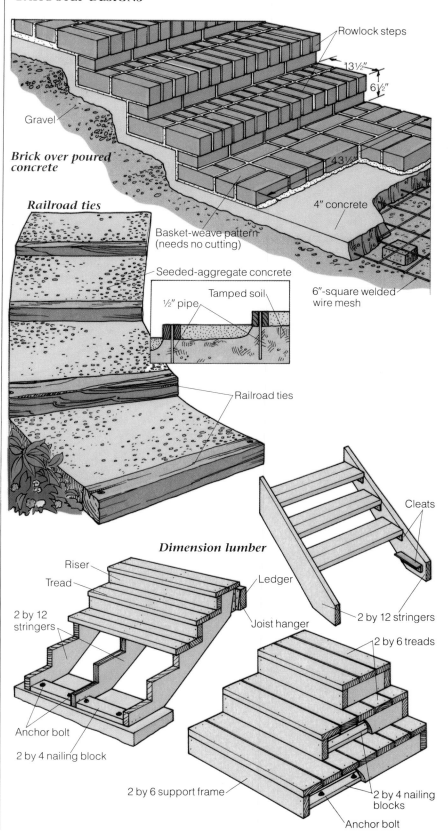

BASIC STEP DESIGNS

Rowlock steps

13½"

6½"

Gravel

43½"

Brick over poured concrete

4" concrete

Railroad ties

Basket-weave pattern (needs no cutting)

Seeded-aggregate concrete

6"-square welded wire mesh

Tamped soil

½" pipe

Railroad ties

Dimension lumber

Cleats

2 by 12 stringers

Riser

Tread

Ledger

2 by 12 stringers

Joist hanger

2 by 6 treads

Anchor bolt

2 by 4 nailing block

2 by 6 support frame

2 by 4 nailing blocks

Anchor bolt

WALLS

A garden wall can bestow privacy, muffle street sounds, frame a view, or simply set off a colorful flower bed.

Wall options range from brick and stone to concrete block and cast concrete. Block is simplest to install; it also makes a great base for plaster, brick, or stone (see pages 82–83). Poured concrete is more difficult: reserve this for very low walls.

A strong foundation or footing is the key to a strong wall. You'll find guidelines on pages 64–66, plus pointers on design, reinforcement, and mortar.

The instructions that follow apply to short walls — those up to about 3 feet. Above that, you'll probably need extra reinforcing, and a permit and/or engineer's report may be required. Be sure to check.

WALL-BUILDING BASICS

Before you build a garden wall, you need to be clear about what you want it to do. Walls can define space, edit views, screen out wind and noise, and hold back earth. Fences can serve many of these functions, but walls perform them with a sense of greater permanence—some of the world's oldest structures are walls.

Once you've defined the purpose of your wall, you can more meaningfully calculate its placement and dimensions. You'll also need to choose materials with which to build it, keeping in mind that coordinating a new wall with existing materials and with the style of your home will probably look best.

You may also be coordinating your wall with new paving. In general, the same rules apply for grading and drainage (see pages 6–7). Retaining walls (ones that hold back soil) require additional planning; see pages 90–93.

Consider the Codes

Before beginning any wall, ask your local building department about regulations that may apply to your project. These will specify how close to your property line you can build, how high you can build, what kind of foundation you'll need, whether or not the wall will require steel reinforcing, and more. Building officials can be of great assistance in steering you right. Constructing your project to their standards is cheap insurance; it assures you of structural integrity.

In the past, building departments were not especially concerned with non-load-bearing walls (walls that carry only their own weight), but in this era of litigation, things have changed. Many municipalities now require a building permit for any masonry wall more than 3 feet high. Some, especially in seismic areas, may also require that the wall be approved by an engineer. Be sure to check.

The Building Blocks

Among the typical materials for garden walls are the various kinds of masonry block, uncut stone, and poured concrete. Examples of walls made of these materials appear on the following pages. You'll also find step-by-step instructions for each option.

In addition to the basic block units, you'll need to make the acquaintance of several other wall components.

Mortar. This is the bonding agent that holds masonry units together. It has several more functions: it seals

A FORMULA FOR FOOTINGS

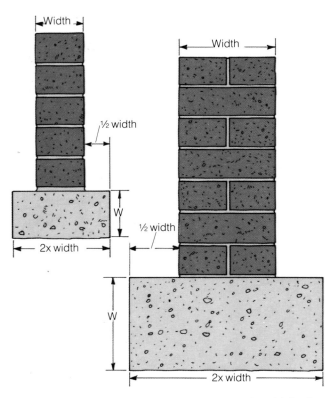

Typically, concrete wall footings are twice the width of the wall and at least as deep as the wall is wide. In cold-weather areas, extend footings below the frost line. Also add 6 inches to trench depth for gravel base.

out wind and water, compensates for variations in the size of masonry units, anchors metal ties and reinforcement, and provides various decorative effects, depending on how the joints are tooled.

Grout is mortar that is thin enough to pour. It is used to fill cavities in masonry walls, such as the cells of concrete blocks (see pages 81–83) or the space inside a brick wall.

For details on mixing and working with mortar, see page 67.

The footing. Regardless of the type of wall you plan to raise, you will have to provide it with a solid foundation, or footing.

Poured concrete is about the best footing you can provide for a wall because it can be smoothed and leveled better than most other materials. The procedure for installing a concrete footing is similar to that for pouring a concrete walk or patio (see pages 25–29).

Usually, footings are twice the width of the wall and at least as deep as the wall is wide, but consult local codes for exceptions to this rule of thumb.

For very low walls (no more than 12 inches high) or for low raised beds, you can lay the base of the wall directly on tamped soil or in a leveled trench.

Reinforcement. In most cases, a freestanding wall more than 2 or 3 feet high should have some kind of reinforcement to tie portions of the wall together and prevent it from collapsing. Before you proceed too far in your planning, check requirements with your local building department.

Steel rods, or rebar (short for reinforcing bar), can provide either horizontal or vertical stiffening. When laid with the mortar along the length of a wall, steel helps to tie different sections of a wall together. Placed vertically (for example, between double rows of brick, or within the hollow cores of concrete blocks), rebar adds vertical strength that can keep a wall from toppling of its own weight.

Special steel ties of various patterns are made for reinforcing unit masonry and attaching veneers to substructures. Two of the most common are shown in the drawing at right.

Pilasters. Vertical columns of masonry, called pilasters, can be tied into a wall to provide additional vertical support. Many building departments require their use at least every 12 feet. Also consider placing pilasters on either side of an entrance gate and at the ends of freestanding walls. These elements contribute

WALL REINFORCEMENT

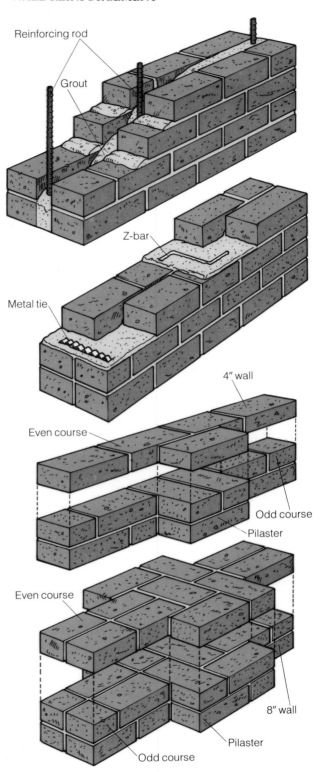

Reinforcing rod (top) strengthens footings and walls. Metal ties and Z-bar (center) help reinforce masonry units and veneers. Pilasters (bottom) provide additional vertical support; successive courses overlap.

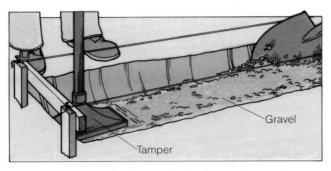

First prepare base for footing by leveling and tamping bottom of trench and adding 6-inch layer of gravel.

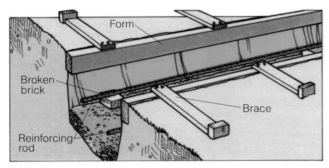

Build forms with 2-by lumber, stakes, and braces. Set any reinforcing rods on broken bricks or other rubble.

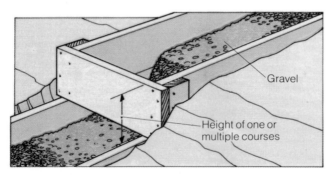

Optional stepped form handles slopes; step height equals one or more courses of brick, block, or stone.

Pour concrete and screed it level with top of forms. Then insert any vertical reinforcing rods into concrete.

visual interest and break up the monotony of a long stretch of wall.

When you're planning the foundation of your wall, don't forget to take pilasters into account. The wall's footing will have to be twice the width of the pilasters.

Building a Footing

Except for a dry stone wall, it's best to use concrete for the footing of a masonry wall. From an appearance standpoint, it is usually best to keep the surface of the footing just below the surface of the ground. This will make the wall seem to rise out of the ground, rather than rest on top of it.

Lay all footings on a 6-inch-deep gravel bed dug deep enough so that the bottom of the footing sits below the frost line in your area. You may need to add reinforcing rods to the footing; if so, decide on the type of reinforcement you'll use before you pour the concrete.

Digging the trench. Lay out the entire course of the wall, marking the corners with stakes. Outline a trench that's the same as the desired dimensions of the footing by building batter boards (shown at left) of equal height at each corner and stretching a mason's line between opposite batter boards. As you dig, the lines will serve as a reference for checking depth.

Dig a straight-sided trench, level the bottom, and tamp it firmly. Shovel in gravel for the base, making sure the top of the gravel layer lies below the frost line. To guide the screed, build a simple wooden form, shown at left; if the soil is too soft to allow vertical sides in the trench, let the form extend down to the top of the gravel. You can also use the technique for wood edgings to build the form; see pages 8–9 for details.

Stepped forms allow you to manage level changes on sloped lots. Curved walls require curved forms, fashioned from kerfed plywood, hardboard, or benderboard (see page 26).

Pouring concrete. Pour the concrete directly into the trench, tamping it with a shovel as you pour. Screed the surface with a piece of wood to make it flat and level. Before the concrete hardens, insert any vertical reinforcing rods you're using.

Let the concrete cure by covering it with a plastic sheet for 2 days. Then you can remove any forms and begin working on the wall.

For more information on pouring concrete, see pages 25–29.

Mixing Mortar

If your plans call for permanent masonry structures, chances are good that you'll be adding mortaring to your do-it-yourself résumé. Here's a quick course to get you started.

Mortar recipes

Mortar recipes vary according to the intended use, but the ingredients are always the same: cement, lime (or fireclay), sand, and water. The cement binds the sand with the building units; lime or fireclay is added to lend workability to the mixture; and the sand helps minimize shrinkage and cracking.

For most jobs, a good all-around mix consists of 1 part portland cement, ½ part hydrated lime or fireclay, and 6 parts sand. This is a good approximation of Type N,

the most common type for general use. Type M, used for paving and other below-grade installations, consists of 1 part portland cement, ½ part lime or fireclay, and 3 parts sand.

You can make your own or buy more expensive ready-to-mix mortar, sold by the bag at building supply stores. Though brand recipes vary, most manufacturers produce a mortar similar to Type N. If your job is small, ready-mix may be your best bet.

Mix it well

Small amounts of mortar can easily be mixed by hand. You'll need a wheelbarrow or similar container and a hoe. Mix the sand, cement, and lime well before adding water. Hoe the dry ingredients into a pile, make a hole in the top, and add some water; mix; then repeat the procedure. Mix only enough to last you about 2 hours; more than that is likely to be wasted.

Ready for use, your mortar should have a smooth, uniform, granular consistency; it should spread well and adhere to vertical surfaces, but not smear the face of your work. Add water a little at a time until these conditions have been fulfilled.

If your job is large, you may wish to rent a power mixer.

Throwing a mortar line

For bricks and other masonry units of similar size, you'll need to learn to throw a mortar line—an even bed of mortar several bricks long. Here's how the pros do it.

A wheelbarrow is ideal for mixing mortar. Blend dry ingredients first, make a hole, and fill it with water. Hoe dry ingredients toward center to blend.

Using a pointed trowel, throw a mortar line several bricks long. Once spread, furrow with trowel point as shown.

Place one or two shovelsful of mortar on a mortar board—a piece of plywood about 2 feet square will do. Load your trowel (a 10-inch trowel holds the right amount for brickwork) by slicing off a wedge of mortar and scooping it up. Give the trowel a shake to dislodge the excess.

Now comes the tricky part—throwing the line. Essentially, it is a two-part motion. As you bring your arm back toward your body, you rotate the trowel, depositing the mortar in an even line about 1 inch thick, 1 brick wide, and 4 or 5 bricks long.

Once the line is thrown, furrow it with the point of the trowel, using a stippling motion. The furrow ensures that the bricks are bedded evenly and will cause excess mortar to be squeezed out to either side as the bricks are laid.

BRICK WALLS

Undulating brick wall leads to gently rising steps. Combination of used and flashed brick—with an occasional stone—sets off informal curves. Landscape architect: Woodward Dike.

For a beginning mason who has never built a wall, bricks are an excellent material to start with. They are easy to handle and place, and their uniform size makes planning the job simpler. The small size of brick units does mean that there will be more units to lay than if you use, say, concrete blocks, but you'll soon establish a rhythm that makes the process enjoyable and even relaxing.

Brick Types

Bricks come in a wide range of colors, textures, and strengths. The photos and text on pages 10–14 will help you evaluate the options.

Basically, bricks fall into two categories: common brick and the more expensive face brick. Common brick is less consistent in size, color, and texture than face brick. Face brick is made of specially selected materials and fired at a higher temperature, which makes it stronger. Common brick is often used for paving. Face brick is excellent for formal walls.

For areas with severe climate variations, especially where the bricks will be exposed to heavy rain and frost, choose SW (Severe Weathering) grade.

Designing a Brick Wall

Brick walls can be run in a straight line or—because the building unit is small—follow a gentle curve. Angling each brick a little produces a slightly curving or serpentine structure that is actually stronger than a straight wall. Bricks can also be staggered to leave open spaces in the wall to allow for air circulation or give a more open, screening effect.

Most bricks are made in modular sizes—that is, the three dimensions are simple multiples of one another. This allows two headers (bricks running across the thickness of the wall), or three rowlocks (headers turned on edge) to equal the length of a stretcher (a brick running along the length of a wall).

Formal raised bed, built from face brick, elevates an Indian laurel fig tree and increases landscape interest. Double corner at right keeps planter from projecting too far out at house corner. Design: The Peridian Group.

Protruding headers and pop-out stretchers add textural interest to this brick backdrop. Modular bricks allow all sorts of patterns, as long as divisions are simple multiples. Before building, be sure reinforcing is adequate.

Brick Walls **69**

Throughout the 5,000 or so years that brick walls have been constructed, masons have developed patterns, or bonds, in which bricks can be laid. Six common bonds are illustrated on the facing page. You can, of course, design your own bonding pattern, using the size of the bricks as your module.

Before you settle on a bonding pattern, though, determine what kind of reinforcing, if any, will be required by local codes. Some bond patterns accommodate steel rods more readily than others.

Headers and stretchers combine to form a handsome, formal structure with screen openings. Architect: Robert Mowat Associates.

Walled patio seems right out of Europe, with common bond and whitewash finish. To achieve an "old" look, build a wall and splash on thick paint or plaster, then remove part of it. Or use new "used" bricks. Original landscape design: Thomas Church. Landscape architect: Delaney & Cochran.

HOW TO BUILD A BRICK WALL

Laying up a brick wall is exacting work. Plan carefully, and don't rush. A flaw in workmanship will not only be visible but, more importantly, will weaken the wall. Choose your pattern, lay your foundation, and work from the ground up and from the ends (or corners) inward.

Bond Patterns

Over the years, many brick patterns have evolved. The ones most frequently used are shown at right.

■ *Running bond* is easy to lay. It's most often used for veneers and single-thickness partitions. Double thicknesses should be linked with metal ties (see page 65).

■ *Common bond* resembles running bond, but includes a row of headers every five courses or so.

■ *English bond,* commonly used in England for structural work, forms very strong all-masonry walls. To use this bond, simply alternate rows of headers and stretchers.

■ *Flemish bond* alternates headers and stretchers in each course. It is both decorative and structural.

■ *Rowlock bond* is a variation of Flemish bond, but alternating headers and stretchers are set on their sides. This provides strength and saves bricks.

■ *Stack bond* is usually used for decorative effect in veneers (see pages 82–83). Because there is no overlapping, it is a weak bond. Don't use it for structural work.

Basic Building Steps

Though you can build brick walls in many shapes and sizes, the easiest to build is a straight, freestanding one. You'll find general design tips below; for step-by-step instructions, see pages 72–73.

Since walls more than a foot high must usually be two bricks thick, the wall is built in two tiers. In effect, it's two 4-inch-thick walls built side by side and connected by bricks laid crosswise to give support to the two half-walls.

This wall is built on the common bond pattern. Headers (bricks running perpendicular to the wall's length) and stretchers (bricks running parallel to the wall's length) are combined in a particular pattern in each course. In this wall, header courses act as reinforcement (usually, steel is not required for low walls).

If your wall will turn corners, be sure to read the instructions for building corners on page 73 before you start.

BONDS FOR BRICK WALLS

Running bond

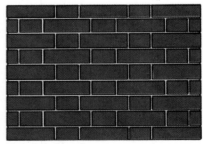
Common bond

English bond

Flemish bond

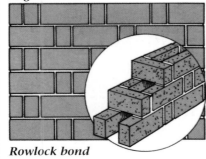
Rowlock bond

Stack bond

Poured concrete is recommended for your wall's footing (for instructions, see page 66), which should cure for about 2 days. Distribute your bricks along the job site. Unless they're already damp, hose bricks down several hours before you begin.

Laying a dry course. To begin building, snap a chalk line to mark the location of the wall's outer edge on the footing. Be sure the wall is centered on the footing. Lay a single dry (unmortared) course of stretcher bricks along the chalk line the full length of the wall, allowing ½-inch spaces for mortar joints. (Using a plywood scrap as a spacer speeds the process.) With a pencil, mark the joints directly on the footing, as shown below. Remove the bricks.

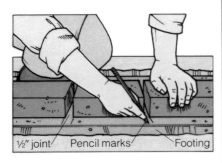

½" joint   Pencil marks   Footing

Laying the first bricks. Spread mortar (see page 67) along the footing and lay the first brick. Butter (mortar) one end of the second and third bricks and set them in place, using your pencil marks as guides. Check that bricks are level and tap them gently into place with the handle of the trowel.

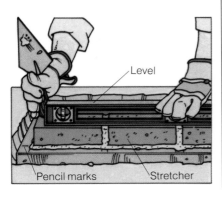

Level

Pencil marks   Stretcher

Beginning the backup course. Lay a course of three backup bricks alongside the three bricks already in place. (There's no need to mortar the joint between courses.) Make sure that the courses are at the same height and that the wall's overall width equals the length of one brick.

Beginning the header course. Next, you'll need to cut two ¾ bricks. Using a brick set, score and then cut the bricks as shown on page 16.

Use the ¾ bricks to begin the first header course. Mortar them in place. Applying mortar as shown below, add four header bricks across the width of the wall.

¾ brick

Backup course

Completing the lead. Continue laying bricks until the lead is five courses high and looks like steps. Note that the fourth course begins with a single header rather than two ¾ bricks. Check to see that all surfaces are straight, level, and plumb.

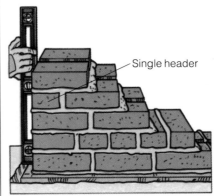

Single header

Build another lead at the other end of the footing, following the same procedure.

Filling in between leads. Stretch a mason's line between the leads, and begin laying bricks from both ends toward the middle, course by course.

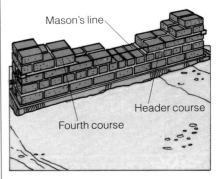

Mason's line

Header course

Fourth course

Keep the line ¹⁄₁₆ inch away from the bricks and flush with the top edges of the course being laid. Double-check your work with a straightedge, since the line will sag if the wall is very long.

If a brick should slip out of place before the mortar has set, scrape out the mortar bed, apply fresh mortar, then reseat the brick.

Closing the top course. Mortar both ends of the closure brick (the last one) in each course, and insert it straight down. Mortar should be squeezed from the joints.

Going higher. To continue upward, build new five-course leads and fill in between them. Check your work often with a straightedge and level. Also sight down the wall periodically to make sure it is true.

Setting the cap. You can cap your wall in many ways; the simplest is a row of header bricks on edge—rowlocks. Lay a dry course first, allowing space for mortar joints. If the last brick overhangs the end of the wall, mark it, score along the line marked, and cut off the excess. Place it three or four bricks from the end, where it will be less noticeable. Remove the bricks, spread mortar along the top of the wall, and begin laying the bricks. Thoroughly mortar the face of each brick and check joint thickness as you go.

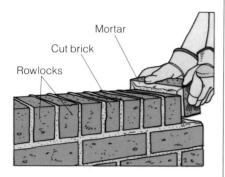

Finishing joints. Smoothing or "striking" the joints creates a finished appearance and helps bond bricks together, sealing the wall against moisture. If you live in a freezing or rainy climate, use a concave joint, weathered joint, or a V-shaped joint, as shown below.

The mortar in the joints is ready to finish when pressing on it with your thumb leaves a slight indentation. Tool the joints as you go so the mortar doesn't harden first. Run a jointer (see page 18) or a similar tool along the horizontal joints. Then draw the tool along the vertical ones. Slide your trowel along the wall to remove excess mortar. When the mortar is well set, clean the entire wall with a stiff broom or brush.

Building Corners

To build a brick wall with corners, you use the same techniques as for a straight wall. After laying out square corners, you begin by building up the corner leads. Fill in between the leads as described on the facing page.

Snap chalk lines on the footing for the wall's outer edges. To make sure the corners are square, use the triangulation method (see page 7).

After making a dry run for the entire wall, spread mortar and lay the first brick exactly in the corner, lining it up with the chalk lines. Then lay two bricks on each arm of the wall, making sure they're straight and level. Spread mortar and lay the backup course in the same way (see below). Don't disrupt the outer course and don't mortar the joints between the courses.

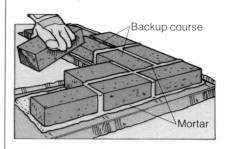

Check for level; then start the header course. Cut two bricks into ¾ and ¼ closure pieces. Lay them as shown below and finish the lead header course. Complete the lead with three stretcher courses, alternating the positions of the corner bricks. Then you're ready to finish the wall between the leads.

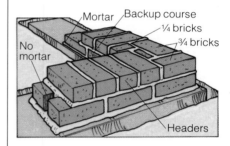

Cleaning Up

Plan to keep the wall moist for a few days. After two or three weeks, you can clean off any mortar stains or traces of white efflorescence (white stains produced by excess water rising to the surface of the brick) that appear on fresh brickwork.

Prepare a solution of 9 parts water and 1 part muriatic acid and apply it with an old rag. Be sure to wear rubber gloves and safety goggles for protection against the acid. Scrub the surface with a stiff brush if necessary. Wash the wall thoroughly with a hose. If the solution comes in contact with your skin, rinse thoroughly and wash with a solution of water and bicarbonate of soda.

TYPES OF MORTAR JOINTS

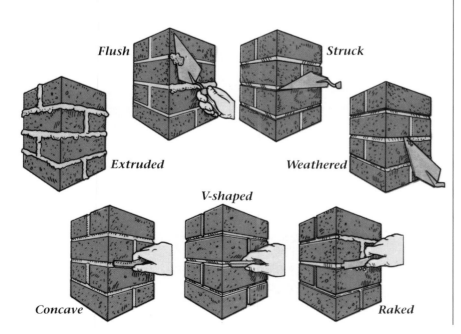

Here are two ways to add interest to concrete walls. The garden wall below was sponge-painted with subtle colors, much like the popular method used for interiors. The angled planter beds at bottom combine plaster and paints. Just for fun, teacups were set into wall. Landscape architect, bottom photo: Delaney & Cochran.

CONCRETE WALLS

Where strength and workability are important, cast concrete is a great material for a wall. With it, you can build a masonry wall of almost any shape or size. Curve it, pour it in a V-shape, or square it up.

The appearance of poured concrete is limited only by your ingenuity. Early modern architects often played up the visual interest of its texture, doing little to conceal the surfaces created by rough construction forms.

If such a raw look doesn't suit you, you can build your construction forms of lumber that has a pronounced and attractive grain. Or you can give formed concrete a smoother finish by whisk-brooming it with a soupy mixture of 3 parts fine sand and 1 part cement. You can also wash or sandblast a wall to expose the small stones in concrete aggregate, or embed rocks and stones in plain concrete's exterior.

Concrete walls can be surprisingly colorful. Chemical stains, tinted plasters, and concrete paints offer almost unlimited options for customizing colors.

The benefits of poured concrete are many. Be aware, though, that casting a concrete wall is no Saturday afternoon job for the casual do-it-yourselfer. Constructing the forms will probably consume more than half of the total time needed to build the wall—more so for curved or sharply angled walls. And the results of a mistake in form-building can be disastrous!

Your building department may require you to reinforce the concrete with steel. Check before starting your project.

Short concrete retaining walls gained graphic appeal from soft coloration and vertical stamping created by rough form boards.

Mortar-streaked wall secludes backyard, screening out neighboring houses. Concrete was "sacked"— surfaced with high-cement plaster mix—to blend new with existing surfaces. Landscape architect: John M. Bernhard.

HOW TO CAST A CONCRETE WALL

Pouring concrete is almost anti-climactic after you have spent the time and effort it takes to build forms adequate to hold it while it sets. A concrete wall can be poured in sections, but each section must be completed before the work stops. A stop-and-go operation could result in air pockets or other faults that would weaken the wall.

For a low, lightweight wall, you could pour the foundation at the same time as the wall. However, for most walls you'll need to pour a separate footing that is keyed on the surface for stability (see drawing at right).

Choosing a Concrete Formula

On page 25, you'll find a formula for making concrete from bulk materials. But for more ambitious jobs, consider the benefits of ready-mix. A ready-mix truck could fill the entire form in one load, provided you have enough manpower to work the concrete.

Constructing Forms

Following are instructions for building forms for a wall (no more than 3 feet high) to be poured on a cured footing (see page 66). If you'd rather not build your own forms, you may be able to rent prefabricated ones—check the yellow pages under "Concrete Construction Forms."

Building a form. Forms for straight walls (see the drawing below) are made up of ½-inch or ¾-inch exterior plywood sheathing, 2 by 4 studs,

FOOTING & FORMS

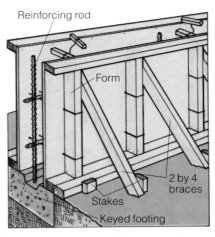

Ready for concrete, forms are staked and braced atop a keyed footing. Tie reinforcing bars to footing bars (as required); overlap them, and secure in several places with wire.

spreaders, wire ties, and (for thicker walls) wales. You'll also need bracing, crosspieces, and stakes to anchor the forms in place.

Each form should be a workable length (8 feet is convenient) and as high as you'd like the finished wall to be. Advisors at your local building department can tell you if wales are advisable for your project; they can also tell you how many you'll need and where to position them.

Make spreaders of 1 by 2s or 2 by 4s; cut them the same length as the finished thickness of your wall, and make enough so you can install them about every 2 feet, horizontally and vertically.

Cut wire ties (8- or 9-gauge iron wire) long enough to encircle opposite studs (or opposite wales, if used), allowing several additional inches for twisting at the ends. Mark and drill a ⅛-inch tie hole in the sheathing along both sides of each stud, near the top and bottom.

Tilt two sections upright on the footing, face to face, and spaced at wall thickness; tack the tops with several crosspieces to hold the sections in place. Thread a tie through the

TWO FORM DESIGNS

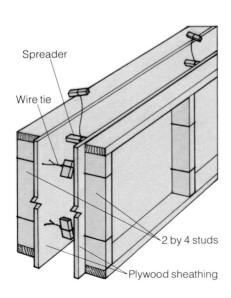

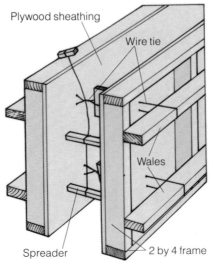

form and around the opposite stud or wale, and twist the wire ends together. Near the tie, wedge a spreader between the sections of the form and, if necessary, hold it in place.

Now put a stick between the two wires inside the form and twist them (as shown below) until they are tight and the spreader is wedged securely between the form sections. Remove the stick and repeat until all spreaders and ties are in place. You'll have to remove the spreaders as the pour is made, so tie long pull wires to any that will be out of reach, and hang the wires over the form's top.

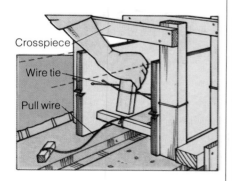

Add sections to this initial one to make up the entire wall form. Butt the sections and nail through the adjacent 2 by 4 studs. To confine the concrete, cleat in stop boards at the ends of your forms (see drawings at right).

Preparing forms. A form must be plumbed and tied in place—it has to stay put during the pour. Nail the bottom to stakes driven in the ground. Lateral movement is prevented by 2 by 4 braces.

If you are using reinforcing rods, tie them into any foundation reinforcing. Generously overlap them, and secure them in several places with wire.

Just before pouring the concrete, coat the inside surfaces of the form with a commercial releasing agent or with motor oil; this will make it easier to remove the forms.

Pouring the Concrete

With footing and forms in place, you're ready to cast a wall on top. Here's how.

Pour and tamp the concrete. Follow the same procedure you used to pour the footings, but take extra care. If you want a smooth finish, be sure to work the concrete well up against the sides of the form. Pour and tamp concrete in 6- to 8-inch layers, pulling out the spreaders as you go and working the concrete in and around the reinforcing bars.

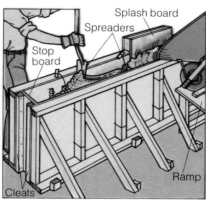

Strike, float, and trowel. Strike off the top of the forms as you did for the footing. Follow with a wooden float and, if you want an extra-smooth surface, finish with a steel trowel.

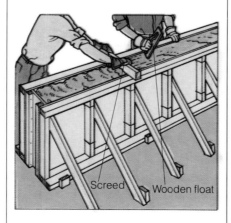

Or consider using a cap. When you've filled the forms close to the top, you can set anchor bolts in the

concrete to hold a wooden cap in place after the forms are removed. Or cast a flared cap atop the rough wall after removing the wall forms, as shown below.

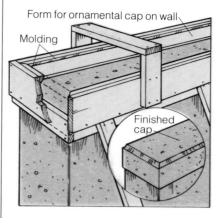

Cure it. Cover and cure the wall for 4 days, unless you intend to texture the wall surface (see below).

Textured Surfaces for Concrete Walls

If you're not satisfied with the "plain vanilla" look of a smooth, cast-concrete wall, you can create a more highly textured surface by using either of the methods outlined here.

Exposed-aggregate surface. First, spray the forms with a special retardant that delays the hardening of the outside layer of concrete. The forms are removed early, and the surface is scrubbed and hosed or sandblasted (not usually a do-it-yourself technique) to reveal the aggregate. The time of form-stripping is critical, so be sure to consult an expert.

Stone-in-concrete. First used by Frank Lloyd Wright, this technique produces a rugged surface and saves on concrete. Selected clean stones are placed against the forms as the pour proceeds; their faces are revealed when the forms are removed. Sometimes it's necessary to chisel away some of the concrete from the faces of the stones.

Concrete blocks make strong, easy-to-assemble walls. Standard blocks are 8 by 8 by 16 inches, with both plain and decorative (split or slump) faces. A whole range of other sizes and blocks complements the basics. Glass-block systems (upper left), with corner clips and other aids, make this material newly accessible for do-it-your-selfers.

BLOCK WALLS

For fast, inexpensive masonry wall construction, it's hard to beat concrete blocks. These rugged units make strong decorative and structural walls, and working with them is comfortably within the capacity of the do-it-yourselfer.

Concrete block is usually much less expensive than brick or stone. It's also generally considered less attractive than those materials. This is not a problem if you use the block wall as a core over which a coating of brick or stone is applied as a veneer (see pages 82–83). Or add plaster over a concrete-block core, opening up a new realm of colors and textures.

Kinds of Concrete Block

The large size of concrete blocks—8 by 8 by 16 inches is standard—makes for rapid progress in building. Most walls can be built with only one thickness of block—an advantage that helps compensate for the blocks' rather cumbersome size and weight.

Basic block. In addition to the 8-inch-wide standard size, blocks come in 4-, 6-, and 12-inch widths. Consider these if your wall is to be very low or if you want a massive effect.

Two weights of block are available. Standard blocks are molded with regular heavy aggregate and weigh about 45 pounds each. Lightweight, or cinder, blocks are made with special aggregates and weigh considerably less. Either type is suitable for most residential projects.

Whatever the size and weight of the standard block, a whole series of fractional units is likely to be available to go with it. In addition, the standard block itself will probably be found in at least stretcher and corner forms (see page 81). With a little planning and care in assembly, you'll never have to cut a block.

Decorative block. Most manufacturers make a variety of decorative blocks designed to produce surface

Glass-block accent wall spills cheery morning sunlight onto this colorful sideyard patio. Newly rediscovered, block "windows" allow for a pleasing combination of light and privacy. Landscape architect: Delaney & Cochran.

Decorative screen blocks lend visual interest and an open feel to a garden wall. This design is capped with concrete; the color matches wide grout in the flagstone paving.

Block Walls **79**

patterns that catch the play of light, enhancing a wall's appearance.

Some units have patterns cast in relief on their face shells. These sculptured blocks can be combined in various ways to produce overall patterns in a wall.

"Slump" blocks are made with the use of a press that gives them an irregular appearance similar to that of trimmed stone or adobe. Dimensions are somewhat variable, in contrast to most other blocks.

Split-face units are actually broken apart in manufacture and resemble cut stone. Combining several sizes enhances their effect.

Screen or grille blocks are designed to be laid on end, usually in stack bond (see page 71). They form patterned screen walls that admit light and air while still affording some privacy.

Glass blocks represent the opposite end of the masonry spectrum from earthy brick or stone. Popular during the '20s, '30s, and '40s, they are currently staging a comeback. Typically, you can find them in 6- to 12-inch squares, and in clear, wavy, or crosshatch textures. Mortar-bearing surfaces are treated to provide a good bond. Installation can be tricky, but several new products are aimed at do-it-yourselfers.

Estimating Your Needs

To calculate how many blocks to order, make a drawing of your proposed project showing the actual number of blocks per course, as well as the number of courses.

For running bond—the best bond to use with most blocks—every other course would begin and end with a half-block. Since each course is 8 inches high, it's easy to figure the number of courses needed to attain a given height and thus the total number of each block type that you'll need. It's a good idea to order a few extra.

Warm-hued wall blends with rustic wood and garden beds; softly contoured plaster surface was applied to concrete block core. Landscape architect: Arthur Vance & Associates. Landscape contractor: Richard Casavecchia/ Architectural Garden Specialties.

Adobe-like wall of white-painted slump blocks winds around the spa. Four-inch openings were created with half-size blocks. Landscape architects: Jones & Peterson.

BUILDING A BLOCK WALL

Laying concrete block is like laying brick, though it goes much faster. Blocks are available in many shapes and sizes (see pages 78–80). For extra strength, you can fill the blocks' hollow cores with steel reinforcing rods and grout. Check with local building authorities about required reinforcing.

Patterns

Basic bonding patterns for concrete block include running bond, offset running bond, and stack bond. With stack bond, use extreme care in vertical joint alignment, as any unevenness is easy to see in the finished wall.

Or vary block sizes and types to contribute pattern interest. For example, why not add a row or two of slump blocks among standard units?

The Basic Sequence

Before digging the footing trench, lay out a dry course of blocks. Space them ⅜ inch apart, and try to plan the footing so that no block cutting will be necessary. (Should cutting be unavoidable, you can use the method described for bricks on page 16, or rent a special saw for the purpose.)

Now install the footing, following the directions on page 66. When the footing has cured, fit a dry course of blocks on top; allow ⅜-inch joints between blocks for mortar. Mark the position of each block and set it aside. Note that the face shells and webs (dividers) are thicker on one side than the other. Always lay blocks with the thick side up; this gives more surface for the mortar bed.

Use the same mortar you would employ for brick (see page 67), but keep the mix a little on the stiff side—otherwise the heavy blocks may squeeze it out of the joints. Don't wet the blocks before laying them. The stiffer mortar and the lower rate of absorption of the blocks will keep them from drawing too much water from the mortar.

Starting the lead. Lay a 2-inch-thick mortar bed long enough for three or four blocks. Then place the corner block carefully and press it down to form an accurate ⅜-inch joint with the footing. Butter the ends of the next blocks, then set each one ⅜ inch from the previous block. Use a level to align, level, and plumb the lead.

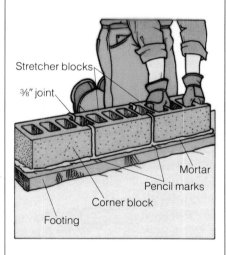

Stretcher blocks
⅜" joint
Mortar
Pencil marks
Corner block
Footing

Completing the lead. Continue as for bricklaying (see pages 72–73), beginning even-numbered courses with half-blocks. For maximum strength, you should mortar both face shells and webs, making full bed joints. When one lead is finished, go to the other end of the wall and build the second lead.

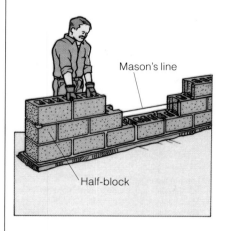

Mason's line
Half-block

Filling in between leads. Lay blocks between the leads, keeping a careful check on ⅜-inch joint spacing. Be sure to check alignment, level, and plumb frequently.

To fit the closure block, spread mortar on all edges of the opening and on the ends of the block, then press it firmly into place.

Closure block

Capping the wall. You can make a simple cap by filling the cores of the top course with mortar. Cover the cores of the next-to-the-last course with ¼-inch metal screening or building paper before laying the top course. Be sure building paper does not interfere with the bond between face shells.

Veneers for Block Walls

To some tastes, block is boring. If this is your predisposition, why not consider disguising a new block wall by veneering over its surface? You can add texture and color by covering it with plastering stucco or by facing it with masonry units such as bricks or stones. Here's how.

Plaster it

Professional landscapers often take advantage of concrete block's low cost and speed of assembly, then use plastering stucco to provide attractive texture and shape. Though plastering is an acquired technique, an accomplished do-it-yourselfer might reasonably tackle a small garden wall.

Buy plaster premixed or prepare your own, mixing 1 part cement with 3 parts sand and up to ¾ part lime. Mix plaster to a plastic (but not runny) consistency, adding water very slowly. To ensure a uniform appearance, use the premixed product for the finish coat.

Plastering stucco creates clean, contemporary veneer atop concrete block base. Apply plaster in two coats; the final coat may be precolored or painted when dry.

Scratch coat. Plastering a new block wall is a two-part operation. The first layer—or scratch coat—should be about ⅜ inch thick. Before applying the plaster, paint the block with a concrete-bonding agent.

Plastering is a workout. You must trowel the mix onto the surface with sufficient pressure for it to bond with the block. On the other hand, it's unwise to overwork the mix once it's applied.

Solid cap blocks, available in various thicknesses, are also a finishing option. Simply mortar them in place on full bed joints, as shown below.

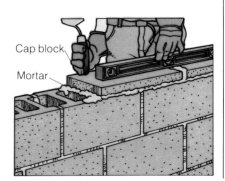

Cap block
Mortar

Finishing the joints. Mortar joints between concrete blocks are finished in much the same way as brick joints (see page 73). The benefits are not just esthetic; finishing also makes the joints weathertight and improves strength.

Wait until the mortar just begins to set; pressure from your thumb should leave a slight indentation. Plan to finish the joints as you go so the mortar does not harden.

A long sled jointer like the one shown at right is best, but a smaller jointer or even a dowel will do. For best strength, use a compacted concave or V-shaped joint. Tool the horizontal, then the vertical joints. Scrape off mortar tags with your trowel.

Sled jointer

As the plaster sets, rough it up—using either a commercial tool or a bunch of wires tied together—to help the finish coat "bite" (that's why this is called a scratch coat).

Finish coat. If the wall is to be painted, use regular gray cement in the plaster mix. If the color is integral, consult with your supplier about coloring oxides, and plan to use a mix with white cement and sand in it.

Apply the finish coat ¼ inch thick, and begin floating when the sheen has dulled. To give texture to the plaster's surface, use a wooden float (see page 18), a steel trowel (with or without notches), a sponge, or a stiff brush.

To cure the plaster, keep it moist for 4 days.

Add brick or stone

Applying a brick or stone veneer to an ordinary concrete-block wall is a good way to dress it up. The result-

Poolside retaining wall was veneered with carefully mortared prairie slate; note smaller "dike" running through larger flagstones. Lighter onyx arch was added for fun. Design: Jonathan Plant & Associates and Steve Marquoit Masonry.

ing wall looks like solid masonry but is accomplished with much less labor and expense.

Placing metal ties. If you're constructing a new wall, first pour the footing, then work on the wall. As you build, place noncorrosive metal wall ties (see page 65) in the mortar joints in every other row of blocks, spacing them 2 to 3 feet apart.

Ties must protrude beyond the blocks; they help secure veneer units.

Attaching stones or bricks. Use mortar to fix the veneer to the core. Bend as many of the wall ties as possible into joints between the stones or bricks. As you build, slush-fill the spaces between the wall and veneer with soupy—but not runny—mortar, filling the spaces completely.

Building in Extra Strength

Block walls taller than 3 feet or so may require reinforcing with steel. This is easily supplied by placing vertical rods in the footing while it is still soft so that they extend up through the block cores, which are then filled with grout or concrete.

If horizontal reinforcing is required, use special bond-beam blocks with cutaway webs to accommodate the placement of horizontal reinforcing rods and grout or mortar. Once the grout sets up around the steel,

the top of the wall becomes a monolithic beam that greatly strengthens the wall. Both vertical and horizontal reinforcing are shown below.

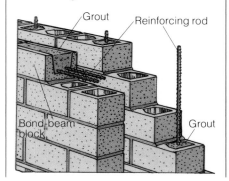

Or substitute special concrete-block reinforcing for the horizontal joints in place of rods. This type of reinforcing, made by welding lengths of heavy-gauge wire together, is available from most block suppliers. Codes generally require it in every course of a screen-block wall.

Longer walls should incorporate pilasters (see page 65). This is easy to do, using full- and half-width blocks. Successive courses should alternate: for example, the placement of 8-inch-wide and 4-inch blocks in one 12-inch course is reversed above.

STONE WALLS

Natural and enduring, stone has been used for wall building for thousands of years. Stonework ranges in appearance from the casual look of rustic rubble walls to the stately formality of fitted ashlar masonry.

Both freestanding and retaining walls can be built either mortared or dry (unmortared). A nice feature of the latter is that you can place soil and plants in the joints as you build, blending the wall into the garden.

In some areas, however, stone is an out-and-out luxury. It takes a lot of time and effort to quarry, trim, haul, and store it—and more to truck it to your yard. Stonework can be difficult work, too; it is probably the most laborious of the masonry techniques. Almost all forms of stone are denser, heavier, and larger than brick, and the shapes of all but the most uniform stones make it difficult to keep large walls plumb and true while maintaining good bonding. Heavy stones are likely to crush their mortar beds—and your fingers, if you aren't careful.

Types of Stonework

As discussed on pages 42–45, stone can be divided into three broad categories according to the way it was formed: igneous, sedimentary, and metamorphic. In addition, there are two broad classes of stonework: rubble and ashlar. Between these extremes you'll find all sorts of roughly squared pieces, where partial trimming of the stones has been done. Cobblestones are one example.

Rubble masonry. The stones used in this type of masonry are often rounded from glacial or water action; examples (often igneous in origin) include granite and basalt river rock and fieldstone. Since they're tough to cut, it's usually easier to search for rocks already the right size. Rubble stone is usually the cheapest available—and if you have a source, sometimes it's free.

Built of sedimentary stone, this garden wall has thin mortar joints, raked to give the appearance of dry-laid construction. Landscape architect: Kenneth W. Wood.

Rugged ashlar stones create a backdrop for a formal garden. Stepped top is capped with concrete; stone is complemented by adjacent brick.

Ashlar masonry. Fully trimmed ashlar stone can be nearly as easy to lay as brick. The flat surfaces and limited range of sizes make formal coursing possible and require less mortar than does rubble work. For a less formal effect, just avoid creating rigid courses.

Ashlar stone is usually sedimentary in origin, with sandstone probably most commonly available. This stone's quality of stratification makes it easy to split and trim. It is softer and less durable than igneous rock, but this is of little concern in non-structural applications. When an igneous stone, such as granite, is cut and trimmed for ashlar masonry, costs are likely to be quite high.

Shopping for Stone

If you calculate the cubic volume of your wall, your dealer can figure the quantity of stone you'll need. Some dealers sell it by the cubic yard, simplifying your order; others sell by the ton. To find the volume of your wall, multiply its height by its width and length. To convert cubic feet to cubic yards, divide by 27.

Try to inspect the stone before you buy it. The rocks should harmonize in color and texture and should show a good range of sizes. For best effect, the face area of the largest stones should be about six times that of the smallest.

Trimmed stones are ordered by width and thickness. Specify the upper and lower limits of length that you will accept.

Fieldstone knee wall frames a private patio, covered with complementary flagstones. Wall stones were mortared atop a base of concrete block. Boulder accents wall's corner. Landscape contractor: Bertotti Landscaping, Inc.

River rocks form striking garden walls, especially in natural settings. These granite boulders were carefully fitted, then set in mortar. Be prepared: rounded surfaces require more mortar than flatter flagstones or fieldstones.

HOW TO BUILD A STONE WALL

Because of the size, weight, and irregular shape of stones, building a dry or mortared stone wall is a very demanding kind of masonry work. But as stonemasons have found throughout history, a careful, methodical approach ensures graceful results.

The key to building an attractive stone wall is careful fitting, whether the wall is constructed with or without mortar. Properly placed stone should produce harmonious and pleasing patterns; the finished structure should appear to be a unit rather than a pile of rocks. As a rule, place stones as they would lie naturally on the ground—not on end or in unnatural positions.

Bonding in Stone Walls

Here, as in brickwork, the principle of overlap is important. As you work, be sure that vertical joints are staggered; there should always be an overlap with the stone above and the one below. Keep in mind the stonemason's basic rule, "one stone over two, two over one."

Freestanding walls are usually laid up in two rough wythes (rows) with rubble fill between them. *Bond stones*, equivalent to headers in brickwork (see page 71), run across the wall, tying it together. You should use as many bond stones as possible—at least 1 for every 10 square feet of wall surface.

Most stone walls should slope inward on both surfaces. This tilting of the faces is called "batter" and helps secure the wall, since the faces lean on each other.

The amount of batter depends on the size and purpose of the wall, the shape of stones used, and whether or not the wall is mortared. A good rule of thumb is to plan 1 inch of batter for each 2 feet of rise—more if stones are very round and less if they are well-trimmed ashlar. Mortared walls can get by with less batter, sometimes none.

To check your work, make a batter gauge (see drawing below) from a piece of lumber that's narrow at the base and wide at the top. When using the gauge, keep the outer edge plumb with a level.

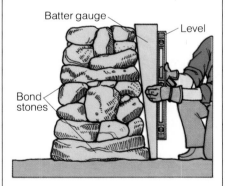

Batter gauge — Level — Bond stones

Building a Dry Stone Wall

Place your stones near the site for convenience while you're building the wall. Use the largest stones for the foundation course. Reserve longer ones for bond stones—long stones that run the entire width of the wall. Also set aside any broad, flat stones to use for the top of the wall.

Foundation course. Begin by laying the foundation stones in a trench about 6 inches deep. First, place a bond stone at the end; then start the two face courses at both edges of the trench. Choose whole, well-shaped stones for the face courses. Fill in the space between the face courses with tightly packed rubble (broken pieces of stone) as shown below.

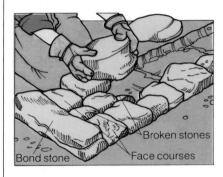

Broken stones — Face courses — Bond stone

Second course. Now lay stones atop the first course, being sure to stagger vertical joints. Select stones that will fit together solidly. Tilt the stones of each face inward toward one another. Use your batter gauge and level on the faces and ends of the wall to maintain proper slope.

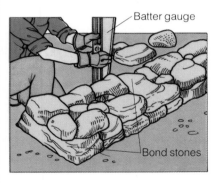

Batter gauge — Bond stones

Place bond stones every 5 to 10 square feet to tie the faces of the wall together. Again, pack the center with rubble and small stones.

Upper courses. Continue in the same manner, staggering the vertical joints from course to course and maintaining the inward slope so gravity will help hold the wall together. Use small stones to fill any gaps, tapping them in with a mason's hammer. Don't overdo it—driving them in too far might dislodge stones you've already set.

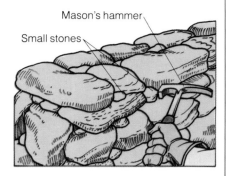

Mason's hammer

Small stones

Top course. Finally, finish the top, using as many flat, broad stones as possible. If you live in an area with severe freezing, you may want to mortar the cap (see inset in drawing below). This will allow water to drain off the wall and help prevent ice from forming between the stones and pushing them apart. Don't rake these joints; tool them flush to prevent water from collecting.

Mortar

Top course

Building a Mortared Stone Wall

Virtually any kind of stone can be mortared to make a stable wall. However, the rounder the stones, the more mortar you'll need. A wall 2 feet thick can safely be built without batter to a height of about 5 feet. Many municipalities require a building permit for any wall more than 3 feet high, so be sure to check.

You'll need a strong footing to support a mortared stone wall. You can build the footings by pouring concrete into wood forms (see page 66) or by filling the footing trench with concrete and stones. If you choose the latter method, be sure the concrete fills the voids between stones. Level off the top of the footings to make a flat surface for the wall's base.

For a 3-foot-high wall, the footing trench should be at least 12 inches deep (in freezing locales, the bottom of the trench must be deeper than the frost line). Allow footings to extend 6 inches beyond the wall's edges on all sides. Ask your building department about reinforcement requirements.

Mortar for stonework. The mortar formula for stonework is richer than that used for brick: mix 1 part cement to 3 or 4 parts sand. You can add ½ part fireclay for workability, but don't use lime (or mortar cement, which contains lime) because it can stain the stones. Keep the mortar somewhat stiffer than for brick.

Depending on the shape of the stone, a wall may be as much as one-third mortar because of the joints and voids. To plan for this, construct a small section of the wall, note the amount of mortar required, and use this as a guide for the rest.

First course. Before you start building the wall, make sure your stone is clean and dry (dirt and moisture interfere with the bond).

To trim an awkwardly shaped stone, chip away the excess material with a mason's hammer. If you need to cut a stone, use a brick set or chisel and sledge. Score a line completely around the stone, then drive the brick set against the line to break the stone apart. Try to work with the natural fissures in the stone, and always wear safety glasses.

Spread a 1-inch-thick bed of mortar at one end of the footing and set the first bond stone, making sure it is well bedded. Now lay the stones in the first course (see drawing below), spreading a mortar bed as you work.

Mortar

Face course

Footing

Bond stone

Pack joints between stones with mortar, and fill the space between the front and back faces solidly with rubble and mortar.

Additional courses. For each subsequent course, build a mortar bed over the previous course of stones; then set the new row of stones in place just as you did for the first course. Remember to place a bond stone every 5 to 10 square feet and to offset the vertical joints. Work slowly, dry-fitting stones before you spread the mortar.

Mortar

You can save mortar by filling large gaps with small stones and chips. As you work, check alignment and plumb or batter.

Very large stones may squeeze out the mortar from adjacent joints. Preserve joint spacing by supporting such stones on wedges of wood. As the mortar stiffens, pull out the wedges and pack the holes with fresh mortar.

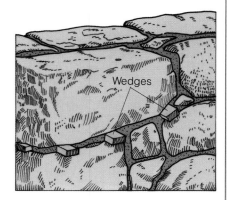

Raking the joints. After you have laid a section, use a jointing tool or wood scrap to rake out the joints to a depth of ½ to ¾ inch. Deeply raked mortar joints enhance the play of light and shadow on the face of the wall. Ashlar stone walls can be tooled as for brick (see page 73).

Cleaning up. Wipe spilled mortar from the stones' faces as you work. After finishing the joints, use a broom or brush to remove crumbs of mortar. Once the mortar has dried, wash the wall with clear water. If this doesn't work, try soapy water followed by a clear rinse. Don't use a steel brush or muriatic acid, either of which could mar the stone.

Broken Concrete

If that old cracked concrete patio or walk must go, why not strike the sledge hammer and a blow for ecology at the same time and recycle it? Broken concrete makes a very attractive garden wall, offering the same informal charm as a wall of stone.

Handle broken concrete in the same way as natural stone: lay the wall up dry or set the broken pieces of concrete in mortar. If you stack the pieces dry, you can grow plants in the cracks.

Concrete pieces also make great paving. To create a casual, cottage-garden look, lay irregularly shaped concrete chunks in a sand bed, with the spaces between them holding ground-cover plantings. Or set them in mortar, filling the joints with contrasting grout. Any technique suitable for flagstone works with concrete, too; for specifics, see pages 46–47.

Like stones, the concrete pieces may have to be shaped. This is best done with a sledge and a brick set or cold chisel.

Whenever you're trimming concrete or stone, wear long sleeves and pants and protect your eyes with safety glasses. The power and velocity with which a heavy tool strikes concrete can send flying small sharp fragments capable of cutting the skin or piercing an eye. Wear gloves when you handle the jagged chunks.

A garden wall is a great way to recycle broken concrete. Laid flat, it resembles rustic stone; chunks turned on edge provide occasional accents.

RETAINING WALLS

If your lot has a sloping area, you may need to include a retaining wall in your garden plan. A retaining wall does what its name implies—it holds back soil, whether earth for a raised planting bed or an entire hillside.

A gentle slope may be tamed with a single low wall or a series of garden steps that hold surface soil in place. A long, steep slope divided into terraces by two or three substantial walls will provide attractive landscaping opportunities.

Code Concerns

A retaining wall acts like a dam, and the pressure exerted on it can be enormous. Clay soil, when saturated, can put literally tons of pressure on the back of a retaining wall. If you live in an area subject to seismic activity, your wall must withstand shock loads as well.

For these reasons, most localities require a permit for a retaining wall; many also specify that walls more than a few feet high be designed and supervised by a licensed engineer. Even for a low retaining wall, it's wise to consult your building department.

Materials

Engineering aside, you can build a retaining wall from any of the materials discussed already. Wood, which is both attractive and easy to work with, is a popular choice. Be sure to use decay-resistant lumber or select pressure-treated stock labeled suitable for contact with the ground.

For low walls, you can lay uncut stones or chunks of broken concrete without mortar or footings. Higher walls need concrete footings and mortared joints for stability. Concrete blocks, bricks (for walls up to about 2 feet), and adobe are also appropriate, especially when reinforced with steel.

Where engineering is critical, poured concrete may be the only solution. You can dress up the wall with a surface veneer (see pages 82–83).

Concrete-block retaining wall units have the look and heft of stone; split-face units were again split in half to give additional rough look. These blocks, though heavy, are ideally suited for do-it-yourselfers. Landscape architect: Lankford Associates.

Rugged wood retaining beds are built from 4 by 6 pressure-treated timbers. Bottom rows were anchored with reinforcing rods; spikes secure upper layers. Inside headers and stretchers are added in crisscross or "crib" fashion, then buried in soil. Landscape designer: Tom Barrett/Environmental Construction.

BUILDING RETAINING WALLS

Building most kinds of retaining walls is challenging work. High ones must be designed sturdy enough to support the enormous weight of the soil they hold back. For this reason, many locales require that an engineer or landscape architect design and supervise the construction of any retaining wall more than 3 feet high or any wall on a steep or unstable slope. Be sure to check.

Grading & Drainage

If space permits, the safest way to build a retaining wall is to locate it at the bottom of a gentle slope and fill in behind it with soil. Or a hill can be held with a series of low walls that form terraces, or with a single high wall. All three methods are shown below.

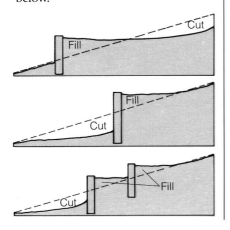

Notice that in each case the retaining wall rests on cut or undisturbed ground, never on fill. If extensive grading is required, it's best to hire a professional.

Hardy, firm-rooted plants that cover well but won't spread too invasively can help hold the soil behind the wall. Plant immediately after completing the wall, while the soil is still soft and easily worked.

Retaining walls must have adequate drainage to prevent water from building up behind them. Surface water can be collected in a shallow ditch dug along the top of the wall. Subsurface water can be channeled into a gravel backfill and conducted away either though a drainpipe buried behind the wall or through weep holes evenly spaced along the wall at ground level. (With weep holes, you may need to employ a ditch along the base of the wall to prevent water from spilling onto the surface below the wall.)

Make sure all drainpipes and ditches are properly sloped so they direct excess water to an appropriate disposal site. For additional details on grading and drainage, see pages 6–7.

Wooden Walls

You can make retaining walls in various sizes from boards or from railroad ties or wood timbers set vertically or horizontally. Use heartwood of redwood, cedar, or cypress, or use pressure-treated lumber (see pages 48–50).

To build a horizontal board wall, first set posts in concrete, spacing them closely and sinking up to half their length into the ground (as required by your building code). Nail the boards to the posts and line them with moisture-proof building paper. Add a decorative cap, if you wish. In the gravel behind the wall, install 4-inch perforated drainpipe. To reinforce these walls, you must run some type of bracing into the slope; one solution is shown above. The soil's

weight on the buried braces helps keep the wall upright.

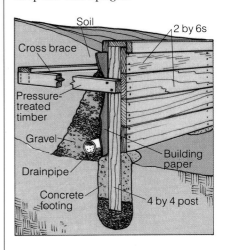

Railroad ties are popular because of their bold, rugged look. To set ties horizontally for a low wall, place them in a shallow trench of hard-tamped earth. Stack ties as shown below. If you need to cut them, use a crosscut saw. Add pipes or reinforcing rods to bolster the walls; or bolt the ties to 4 by 4 posts. Geotextile fabric, secured between ties, serves the same purpose as the bracing shown above. Corners and angles can also add strength.

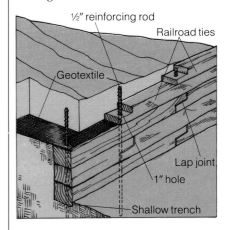

To set ties vertically for a straight or curved wall, soak the cut ends in wood preservative. Set them in the soil so half their length is above the ground. For greater stability, you can set the lower ends in concrete and connect the ties along the back with a continuous strip of sheet metal (such as flashing) fastened with wide-headed nails. Use this technique for short walls only.

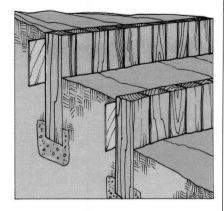

Also consider using pressure-treated timbers in place of railroad ties. If their greenish tinge bothers you, wait a few months, then paint or stain them to your liking.

Dry Walls

A stone or broken-concrete retaining wall laid without mortar is a good choice for a low, fairly stable slope. The crevices between the rocks or concrete pieces can become soil-filled pockets for colorful plantings.

Heavy, uncut stone demands patient work. Fit the stones carefully (their uneven surfaces will help hold them in place), laying them so they tip back into the slope. Set soil between the rocks as you build.

Use a heavy sledge hammer to break concrete into pieces for a wall (be sure to wear safety glasses). Lay the rubble, smooth side down, in courses, staggering the joints.

Unit Masonry Walls

Walls built of masonry units mortared together are good for holding steep or unstable hillsides.

Brick, adobe, and stone are suitable materials for low mortared walls. Ask your building department about requirements for reinforcing. For advice on construction, consult the appropriate sections in this chapter.

For a high wall, concrete blocks are best. The block wall shown below left rests on a footing reinforced with steel rods. The wall itself is built of bond-beam blocks (see page 83), with horizontal reinforcing where needed. Grouting is done by courses. Drainpipes form weep holes for drainage. Capping the wall with mortar and facing it with a masonry veneer enhances its appearance.

Poured Concrete Walls

A poured concrete wall reinforced with steel is the strongest type of retaining wall you can build. But the labor required can make it a costly project.

Poured concrete walls can be either mass walls or cantilevered. A mass wall, such as the one shown below right, relies on its own weight to prevent it from tipping or sliding. The width of the base must be ½ to ¾ of the wall's height. On low walls, steel reinforcing isn't usually required, but a horizontal ⅜-inch rod near the top will add strength.

Cantilevered walls of poured concrete rely on the weight of the earth pressing down on a large footing to hold them in place.

TWO MASONRY WALLS

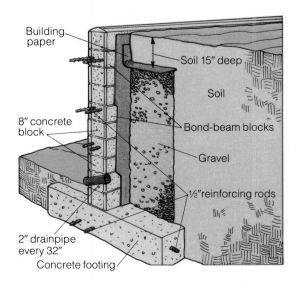

Building paper
Soil 15" deep
Soil
Bond-beam blocks
8" concrete block
Gravel
½"reinforcing rods
2" drainpipe every 32"
Concrete footing

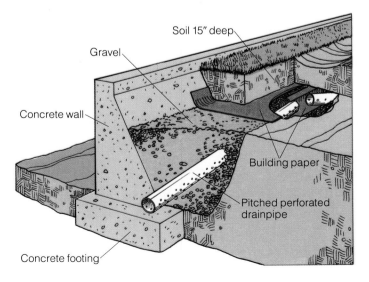

Soil 15" deep
Gravel
Concrete wall
Building paper
Pitched perforated drainpipe
Concrete footing

Raised Beds

A well-designed raised planting bed provides a smooth transition between levels and, as an added advantage, puts plants at a height more convenient for the gardener. Add a wide wall cap, and your planter can double as a bench.

In some cases, the restrictions governing formal retaining walls may also apply to raised beds; however, most planters are simply low walls, rarely more than 12 to 18 inches high.

Materials

Any of the materials suited for retaining walls (see pages 90–93) can be used for raised beds. Wood, brick, stone, and concrete are all prime candidates, depending on your overall landscaping scheme.

Wood is especially versatile. Railroad ties and other large timbers, though somewhat awkward to handle, make attractively rustic walls for raised beds. Unadorned wooden planks and stakes complement nearly any landscape design and are easily adapted to various shapes and sizes. Always remember to use pressure-treated lumber or decay-resistant heartwood of cedar, redwood, or cypress.

Raised beds made of unit masonry are strong and enduring, and can be constructed in many different shapes and styles. A brick-walled bed can lend elegance and distinction to a formal garden scheme. Even a plain concrete-block wall can be dressed up with a veneer of stone or brick. You can also construct raised beds from poured concrete.

Construction tips

Raised beds are usually easy to build. The vertical supporting face acts like a small retaining wall, with one significant difference: a raised bed rarely has to withstand soil pressure comparable to that exerted on most retaining walls. A low, informal bed may not require a footing—though it's always a good idea to use one with mortared masonry. To build a bed from standard dimension lumber, see the photos below.

Drainage is crucial. If the bed is open at the bottom, most excess water will drain out. If it's closed, make small weep holes 2 to 3 inches from the ground, spaced 2 to 3 feet apart. Place a 4-inch layer of crushed rock or pea gravel in the bed before filling it with soil.

To build a wooden unit, first nail short sides of 4- by 10-foot rough redwood bed to corner posts (left). Sides are doubled 2 by 10s; posts are 32-inch 4 by 4s. Next, with ends upside down, nail 10-foot sides to corner posts (center). Set bed right-side up into predug foot-deep holes, then cap the top with redwood 2 by 6s (right).

A tree-form glossy privet grows contentedly alongside a bank of bright impatiens in its small raised planter and rarely sheds messy leaves. Landscape architect: Glenn Herbert.

Index